D0876791

FROM

Cursed

TO

Blessed

Obey God's
Commandments & Live

TAMARA KEELER

© 2022 by Tamara Keeler
All Rights Reserved under the Pan-American
and International Copyright Conventions
Printed in the United States   052222
KJV Bible quoted unless otherwise stated

This book may not be reproduced in whole or in part, in any form or by any means, whether auditory, graphic, electronic or mechanical, including photocopying, recording, or by any information storage and retrieval system now known or hereafter invented, without written permission from the author, except in the case of brief excerpts used in critical articles and certain other noncommercial uses permitted by copyright law. Unauthorized reproduction of any part of this work is illegal and punishable by law.

ISBN: 9798831396171
Imprint: Tamara Keeler

Library of Congress Control Number: 2022910125

For more information please visit:
https://Leansteward.com
Email me: Inbox@Leansteward.com

Table of Contents

Introduction

My life was a disaster before I began to hear and obey God's commandments. My fiancé was a man who wasn't my husband. The relationship was going well as we maintained a Christian relationship to prepare for marriage until I left him, not realizing I would be stuck with a mountain of bills to pay. My car note was six months late, and my house would be foreclosed on any day because the payment was more than two months late. On the other hand, my racist boss at work made me sad and terrified every day. I was so depressed that I had transferred my misery to my youngest daughter. It always broke my heart when I couldn't meet her basic needs, such as paying for her volleyball club. How do you explain to a child that providing food and a place to live was more important than paying for her volleyball club?

On top of that, my kids and I were sick with various ailments ranging from stomach pains, depression, and allergies. I was struggling with obesity and suffering from back pains, being out of breath from walking up a flight of stairs, and having my thighs rub together painfully.

Because all these things were happening at home and at work, I declared bankruptcy. I was cursed even though I was still going to church every Sunday, paying tithes, and helping anyone who needed it.

It wasn't until I started hearing and obeying God's written commandments that my burdens began to lift slowly but steadily. Only a small percentage of those who truly love the Lord have read the entire Bible for themselves. I was among them. I remember reading the bible once in college, but it wasn't for comprehension. It was more like wanting to understand what it was saying. But this time, I read it, or rather, listened to it on YouTube all the way through to ensure comprehension. I was astounded to discover that my life and routines were the opposite of what the word implied.

I stopped going to church after I read the bible. My friends, who had recently joined a church, (after trying for years to get them to come), asked me, "How can you stop going to church after I've finally joined a church?" My transformation can be described in the book of James KJV 1:23-25, it reads, "For if any be a hearer of the word and not a doer, he is like unto a man beholding his natural face in a glass: For he beholdeth himself, and goeth his way, and straightway forgetteth what manner of man he was. But whoso looketh into the perfect law of liberty, and continueth therein, he being not a forgetful hearer, but a doer of the work, this man shall be blessed in his deed."

I no longer had to file for bankruptcy. When I told the bankruptcy lawyer, she thought some agency had tricked me into consolidating my debt. My truck payments were reduced by $300, to an affordable rate. My home didn't go into foreclosure. My daughter's volleyball payments were dropped from $560.90 a month to only $26.50. My eyes are tearing up now, just thinking about how the Lord blessed us and took away the burdens. One of the fellow volleyball club families gifted some of their frequent flyer miles to help my daughter fly with the team to Orlando, Florida, for the National Championships. She only missed a few out-of-town games. The following year, she was recruited to a higher-level national team with a very affordable payment. My daughter now has a 4-year guaranteed volleyball scholarship worth over $100,000 to a Christian college.

My eldest daughter received a scholarship for her first year in college. We don't have to pay anything out of pocket. I was also blessed with a new job and manager at work, and my career and development have taken off. The job matches my passions and fits the cliché, "you'll never work a day in your life."

On top of these life-changing events, our health improved; I lost 100 pounds of weight along with all the strain that comes with being obese. As if that wasn't enough, God showed me that I was still married to the husband of my youth, the father of my daughters. The Lord blessed us to be reunited after more than ten years of being divorced. All of these blessings in just two years of obeying the word. I wish I had started applying God's principles earlier in life.

Being a Christian, studying sermons each Sunday, attending Sunday School, and praying was a lot of effort with minimal results. Nothing changed in my life until I started to know for myself what the word of God said and obeyed it. I couldn't just hear the word and not do what it instructed.

I took a radical approach by literally listening to a chapter of the bible and adjusting my life to what it said. This approach should not be repeated because some things I read in the earlier books of the bible had their meanings explained in later chapters or had been fulfilled, but I was desperate and didn't want to take any chances. Nevertheless, after two years, I can testify that I was blessed indeed.

I also challenge each of you to read aloud or listen to the entire bible for yourself, and afterward, do not walk away from the reflection in the glass or forget what your life looks like in comparison to it, but make small changes to obey what you heard, and you will experience life more abundantly. The following scriptures give evidence to the message that obeying the commandments of the Lord is where the blessing is at.

Exodus 19:5 says, "Now therefore if you will obey my voice indeed and keep my covenant then ye shall be a peculiar treasure unto me above all people for all the earth is mine." Exodus 23:27 says, "For thou shall indeed obey his voice and do all that I speak then I will be an enemy unto thy enemies and an adversary unto thine adversaries." Deuteronomy 11:27 says, "A blessings if ye obey the commandments of the Lord your God. And a curse if you will not obey the commandments of the Lord your God." I Samuel 12:13 says, "If you will fear the Lord and serve Him and obey His voice and not rebel against the commandment of the Lord, then shall both ye and also the king that reigneth over you continue following the Lord your God. But if you will not obey the voice of the Lord and rebel against the commandments of the Lord, then shall the hand of the Lord be against you as it was against your fathers." Jeremiah 7:22-23 says, "For I spake not unto your fathers, nor commanded them in the day I brought them out of the land of Egypt concerning burnt offerings or sacrifices. But this thing commanded I them saying Obey My Voice, and I will be your Elohim, and ye shall be my people. And walk ye in all the ways that I have commanded you, and it shall be well unto you."

Be Who You Were Meant To Be

By Tamara Keeler

Be who you were meant to be
Your words are alive, speak the truth you want to see
Read the law, all you gotta do is believe
Achieve the life, that will be your testimony

Let the light in you work a miracle
Shine bright as a city, and give unto the people
Let go of Fear, you are more than able
Trust only in God, live happily ever after

Why you working two and three jobs to survive?
Your gift will make room for you in the sky
Trust and believe the odds you will defy
All things of God belong to you and I

The world is waiting to see just who you will become
That's why the Father gave you His first-born son
Make a sanctuary in your heart for Him to come
There's only winning when you and Him become one

Chapter 1: Be Who You Were Meant To Be

The words that you speak are alive and have the power to create, facilitate, recruit, build, lift, tear down, heal, or bring peace. You can go from cursed to blessed by using your words to focus on the results that you want to see.

To demonstrate this truth, let's start by reviewing a few scriptures. Genesis 1:3 says, "And God said, Let there be light: and there was light." When God spoke, his word was the one who made there be light. His word is the worker that accomplishes the will of God. Isaiah 55:11 says, "So shall my word be that goeth forth out of my mouth: it shall not return unto me void, but it shall accomplish that which I please, and it shall prosper *in the thing* whereto I sent it." When God speaks, His word will accomplish any task spoken. This is because, as the word of God, that is all He is permitted to do.

Your words manifest reality. If you say things like, "I'm broke, I'm stupid, I'll never get ahead," then you will be broke, stupid, and struggle. If you say things like, "I'm the head and not the tail, I'm blessed when I go in, and I'm blessed when I go out" then you will lead a blessed life. And if you say things like, "I hate...., I can't stand..., I don't forgive...." your words will block love, tolerance, and forgiveness.

Are y'all catching on yet? Your words will bring you a spiritual harvest. God's words are alive and have a name: Jesus. His word was made flesh and dwelt among us. He came unto His own, but His own received Him not, but those who received Him unto them Jesus gave the power of everlasting life. All things were made by Him; and without Him was not anything made that was made. In Jesus was life; and the life was the light of men. And the light shineth in darkness; and the darkness comprehended it not.

The word of God is trying to enlighten you. And He will never stop trying all the days of your life. He said He came to save sinners who were lost. When the father spoke you into existence, he said be fruitful, multiply, and have dominion over the Earth. In His word, Jesus has a responsibility to help us do what the Father has commanded us to do. When we read His word, Jesus, teaches us how to love, forgive, break generational curses, give, who to give to, how to produce a harvest, where to go, where to work, how to heal, how to heal others, how to pray, and how to recognize the path we are to follow. He is fully capable of prospering us, which is the thing that He was sent to do.

In John 14:12, Jesus says, "Verily, verily, I say unto you, He that believeth on me, the works that I do shall he do also; and greater works than these shall he do; because I go unto my Father." Jesus said that you and I would do greater things than Him. I encourage you to speak great things and achieve the dreams that you were meant to achieve.

Which top five things that would make you overjoyed if they improved in the next three months?

1. _____
2. _____
3. _____
4. _____
5. _____

A screenwriter writes the gist of what's happening in a scene. Everyone else gets to interpret what the writer meant visually. For example, a screenwriter can write, "This is the crappiest hotel ever!" It is then the job of the director, the production crew, the sound crew, the costume designers, etc., to produce a set built to look like the crappiest hotel ever. The screenwriter has no business trying to tell the cameraman how to do his job, when he should get a close-up, or from what angle. The screenwriter doesn't hire the actors who will speak those lines. The writer's responsibility is to write, which is why at the end of movies we see a long list of people's names who helped to deliver the final movie creatively.

In comparison, we are like the screenwriter. Our job is to speak the things that we need to be who we truly are meant to be. Our words are like everyone else in the story. Our words are the manager, the producer, the lighting crew, the hiring manager, the recruiter, and everyone else needed to produce the movie. It is not our job to figure out "How" our words are going to accomplish what we said. It is only our job to focus on the "What & The Why."

Jesus is the word of the Father. He was equipped to change water into wine, He called in an abundance of fish during a time of scarcity, he cast out unclean spirits, healed and fed thousands of people, prophesied about the future, and calmed a storm with his word. Yet, he said that you and I would perform greater things. Think big about the solutions to the problems and situations you have found yourself in.

For example, the bible tells a story about a man who was lying by the pool of Bethesda for 38 years, waiting for his healing. All he knew was that other people were quicker to enter the water than him. Jesus told him to rise, take up his bed and walk. The man was thinking about a small solution to solve his problem. He was looking to the water for the healing of his body. But Jesus wanted him to know that if he looked to God instead of to the water, he could not only have healing for his body, he could have healing for his mind, improved finances, a promotion, a new business, a more prosperous business, wisdom, training, acceptance in school, and every spiritual attack against foiled, for all things are possible with God.

Jesus said in John 4:13-14, "Whosoever drinketh of this water shall thirst again: But whosoever drinketh of the water that I shall give him shall never thirst; but the water that I shall give him shall be in him a well of water springing up into everlasting life." Ask yourself if you are looking to the water to bring about your solution, or are you looking to God? Are you looking for a temporary fix that will get you by today but cause you to be back in the same situation next year? Are you looking for a government program that can pay a rent or mortgage payment, or are you looking to the God who gives out palaces? Are you looking to your two or three jobs to keep food in your refrigerator instead of the God who says that if you give to his poor servants, widows, the fatherless, or strangers, then there will be no lack in your home?

Get the truth, which is the light of Jesus inside of you. When situations arise, and troubles come, His truth will spring up like a well of water that you can drink from to cast out lies of the enemy. Quench your thirst with the word of God. Drink His word and give yourself peace in situations that cause anxiety in others. Drink His word to praise Him in times of hardship when other people are sad and don't know what to do. Drink His word and have faith that when you have obeyed His commandments, His word will not return unto Him void but produce what it was sent to do.

What are a few scriptures that confirm that you can have everything on your 3-month list?

_____

_____

_____

_____

_____

_____

_____

_____

The bible says that as children of God, we can have whatsoever we ask for if we ask according to His will. This means that if there is anything that we honestly need to achieve the harvest that we were sent to create, then He will grant us whatever we ask. Question: If God gifted me to be a writer, and I need pencils, notebooks, or a computer to write when I ask for those things according to his will, should I receive them?

The statement said that He would grant you all things to produce a harvest, not just because you were gifted with a gift. A harvest doesn't mean money for you. It means you continued in the work of the Lord by giving to the poor, helping his servants, caring for widows, the fatherless, strangers, having mercy on loved ones in prison, etc. For example, Solomon used his gifts to serve God's people. I Kings 3:9 says, "Give therefore thy servant an understanding heart to judge thy people, that I may discern between good and bad: for who is able to judge this thy so great a people." Hannah spoke a vow to God that she would lend her son to Him if God blessed her with a son. Abraham spoke a vow that if God gave him and his 300 men the victory over five kings to rescue his nephew Lot, then he would pay God tithes of the spoils and not touch any of it for himself.

When we share in the work that Jesus is doing to produce His harvest, we can have all needed resources. This is one reason why John 16:23, Jesus says, "Verily, verily, I say unto you, Whatsoever ye shall ask the Father in my name, He will give it you." When we ask in the name of Jesus, we are indicating that the thing we ask is needed for Jesus to produce His work in us. It's as if we are managing a project account under the name of Jesus. We have authority to charge the account with all things that pertain to the project. Any equipment, supplies, land, salaries expenses, rent expense, insurance, healing, food, or resources needed for the project, are already approved. It is our responsibility to request the resources and manage them.

I just love the transformational story of Mrs. Tabitha Brown, "America's Mom." After years of failed attempts to pursue her fleshly desires of becoming an actress in Hollywood and drawing people to her, she obeyed the voice of God to draw people to Him. She has achieved more success than she could ever imagine. In an Ellen Show interview, Tabitha revealed that God repeatedly told her to "Heal the World" and that "It starts with children." Tabitha understood that if she could get children to open their minds to accept themselves, love others, and give compassion despite their differences. Then, those same children would become adults who accept themselves, loves others, and give compassion. Tabitha's surrender to Jesus and obedience to the work He was doing through her is what propelled her to live out the life she was created to live.

In Luke 16:10, Jesus says, "He that is faithful in that which is least is faithful also in much: and he that is unjust in the least is unjust also in much." Tabitha requested a gift of healing so that she could do the work of the Lord. After receiving that small gift, she started putting forth the effort to do his work. Because

Tabitha was faithful and obedient with the least, God blessed her with more. When we request resources for the project in Jesus's name, we must then use those resources to do his will and show ourselves to be good stewards.

However, many people are using their gifts for personal gain. The book of Numbers tells the story of Balaam, a gifted prophet for hire, who nearly lost his life in the pursuit of a reward. Or when David's misuse of power cost him the life of his newborn son with Bathsheba. And, we can't forget about Gehazi in 2 Kings, who was cursed with leprosy after seeking a reward for assisting in Naaman's healing. These people were filled with the lust of the eyes, the lust of the flesh, or the pride of life.

Nevertheless, God does let His sunshine on the good and the evil alike, and He sends his rain on the just and the unjust. For people like Paul who was used by God in the later half of his life, God granted him power, favor, and intellect even though he used those gifts to murder and persecute believers of God. God just may grant overwhelming blessings to someone working contrary to His will, because, in the end, they will use their fame, their wealth, and everything they have done to serve Him.

Think about how much would it improve your life if you had everything you wrote tomorrow or in your three-month time frame? What do you need that will also further the kingdom of God? A new job to better give back to people? A new home to help a family member live comfortably? Your book published that you know will inspire people to change their lives for the better? These types of things are not just needed for personal joy but also to help others.

For each thing that you need to be improved or changed in the next three months give a reason for why you need it.

I need _____ because _____.

I need _____ because _____.

I need _____ because _____.

I need _____ because _____.

I need _____ because _____.

The Bible talks about not only people who have increased by 30-60-100 fold but also people whose lives have improved by 10,000%. 1 Samuel 2:8 says, "He raiseth up the poor out of the dust, *and* lifteth up the beggar from the dunghill, to set *them* among princes, and to make them inherit the throne of glory: for the pillars of the earth are the LORD'S, and He hath set the world upon them."

Do you understand that you are a pillar of the earth? This is the hidden meaning in the passage. Do you understand that God knows that the very people who the world was made for are the ones who have the least knowledge and are considered poor? Ecclesiastes 10:7 says, "I have seen servants upon horses, and princes walking as servants upon the earth." Doesn't this make you want to cry? But we can get you back to the true you in a few easy steps. Then the true pillars of the world will be set in their place.

"A man's gift maketh room for him, and bringeth him before great men." Proverbs 18:16. Look at the life of Joseph. His gift took him out of prison as a convicted rapist and placed him before the King of Egypt. But I hear many people say that they don't know their purpose. They don't know what they naturally were sent here to do. Try these exercises to help you figure out what you were created to do.

If I could get paid to _____ every day, it wouldn't even feel like I was working.

_____
_____
_____

When I was a kid, I dreamed about being a…………?

_____
_____
_____

It seems like people always seek me out to help them with…………….?

_____
_____
_____

I excel better than others whenever I'm doing …………….?

_____
_____
_____

Random people have always complimented me for being great at…………….?

_____
_____
_____

I've always wanted work doing…………….but it doesn't pay well.

_____
_____
_____

Too many people are miserable doing work that God never gifted them to do. They may naturally love historian work but spend their time as lumberjack. Or they naturally love to draw, but they work as a masseuse. Or God is constantly sending people into their lives to receive the ministry of prayer, but they are settling for driving a semi-truck and do not realize how a gift of prayer could earn them a living.

Let go of the spirit of fear and believe that when God created you and said "be fruitful and multiply", His word can produce the "you" that you were created to be. You may have lived in poverty. God is not poor. You might have been born with a speech impediment. God does not stutter. You may not feel like the smartest one in the bunch. But Wisdom hangs out with God. Do not equate your situation or set of circumstances as His roadblock. Take His situation and plow through your roadblock. Remember these next two scriptures:

- 2 Timothy 1:7, "For God hath not given us the spirit of fear, but of power, and of love, and of a sound mind."

- Philippians 4:19 "But my God shall supply all your need according to His riches in glory by Christ Jesus.

Jesus will never stop trying to reach you. Come into agreement with his efforts and desires for your life. He will keep trying to get your attention, get you to see things from his perspective, and try to straighten the path you are walking on. God's word will try every possible attempt to prosper you. Luke 19:10 says, "For the Son of man is come to seek and to save that which is lost." We have all heard Him say that He will leave the 99 to save the one who is lost. If you are not doing the work you were created to do, you are still lost. Say these words out loud "There's a lot of light left to shine inside of me."

Get that 10,000% improvement in your life by doing the work that further improves this Earth that was created for us. Go as far as you were meant to go. Do you understand what a 10,000% improvement looks like? Suppose someone is a beggar who eats out of the garbage but offers a solution to the problems of today. In that case, that beggar can have more power than the President of this nation, more authority than the Chief Supreme Court Justice, and more influence than the richest Hollywood Star. A 10,000% improvement is how David went from playing crazy and working security for loaves of bread to save his own life to being promoted to the King of Israel. He understood that he was a pillar on the Earth. He understood that his current situation of not having a lot was not his future destiny that God meant for his life. David knew that he had already been anointed as the king. David blessed the Most High God and obeyed his commandments. David let his little light shine on the men who began to follow him.

I would love to see you go from cursed to being as great as you were meant to be. I would love to see you produce the things that bring you great joy. I would love to see you go as far as you were meant to go. Now, this is not some name it and claim it message. You need to position yourself to hear the truth. There are many people who speak good things over their lives, but when their words return to them, they don't recognize it. It's like their eyes are shut, and their ears are closed. The book of Isaiah indicates that many people are cursed because they have put their trust in men or a government program. Jeremiah 17:5-6 says, "Thus saith the LORD; Cursed *be* the man that trusteth in man, and maketh flesh his arm, and whose heart departeth from the LORD. For he shall be like the heath in the desert, and shall not see when good cometh; but shall inhabit the parched places in the wilderness, in a salt land and not inhabited."

What shall we do to position ourselves to recognize when good comes?

#1 We can't put our trust in people.

- This means that if we loaned someone money and they haven't paid us back, we will not get angry. We will trust in God as our provider.

- If our kids' father didn't do his part to help us out, we wouldn't accuse him. We will trust in God as our provider.

- This means if the very people we think are supposed to help us end up turning their backs on us, we won't hold a grudge against them. We will trust in God as our provider.

#2 We can't put our trust in the government.

- This also means that we will not feel hopeless if we get denied for a government program. We will trust in God as our provider.

- This means that we will use the money we have to pay the bills that are due right now and not wait for a program to provide for us.

- This means that we will not be irresponsible with money and go on a spending spree because we are waiting for tax money to save us. Instead, we will do anything and everything in our power to make it right with our creditors and be good stewards of the finances we have been entrusted with.

#3 We won't trust any get-rich-quick schemes.

- This means that we refuse to break God's commandments to provide for ourselves, such as resorting to robbery. We will trust in God.

- This means that we will refuse to gift money to a church's building fund in hopes of receiving an instant return. We will trust in God.

- This means that we will not seek after money by picking up two extra jobs, making ourselves our providers. Nor will we listen to Wall Street preachers who say that our best option is to invest with them. God says that our best option is to invest in the lives of the poor to reap a harvest. We will trust in God as our provider.

To recognize when good comes, we must make God our sole provider. This scripture in the book of Jeremiah is saying that anything contrary to us trusting in God as our provider, is bringing a curse upon us.

I remember waiting in line at the currency exchange carrying a water bill and a gas bill with not enough money to pay both bills. And a thought entered my mind that told me it was best to pay the water bill instead of the gas bill because the energy assistance program could pay the gas bill for me. I rebuked that thought in the name of "I Am That I Am". I understood that by accepting that thought I would have made the program my arm, bringing a curse upon me. I paid the full gas bill instead.

What are some ways you have put your trust in man, family, a non-profit, a spouse, the government, or a program in the past?

_____
_____
_____
_____
_____

There are two things you must do to position yourself to receive the blessings and to recognize when good comes:

#1 Repent of your sins
#2 Read the word of God daily

Even though these two items may seem very simple, they are the most difficult challenge for many people because of how often they are often misunderstood. They sound like two completely different things, but they should work together in such a way that you can't do one without the other. How can you repent of your sins if you haven't read the bible to know what sin is? Many people think that sin is drinking or smoking or going to a nightclub. They think that if they go to church and stop drinking or smoking or hanging out all night, they are now holy. But I have seen more children of God outside of the church than I have inside of the Church.

For example, I met an older woman whose name is Ms. Keeta. Ms. Keeta truly demonstrates the heart of God in giving hot food to anyone who may be hungry and providing clothing to anyone who is half-dressed. She calls to check in with people to see about their needs. She makes it a point to help them with whatever she has in her possession. Ms. Kia wanted to join a church, but she stated that she would not join a church because she still smoked and sometimes used cursed words in her speech. In her mind, smoking and using curse words was a sin that stopped her from becoming Holy like the people in the church.

I can agree with Ms. Keeta that people who attend church have a reputation to not use curse words or smoke. However, they also have a reputation in quite a few other areas as well. Often times, they only see you when church is in session. Those same people may not have any clothing in that church to help someone who is half-dressed. They also might not have any hot food to give away to those who may be hungry. Neither would they stop by your home to learn if there is anything that you are lacking. Other than seeing you in church or sending a bible text to your phone, those people usually have no real connection with you. And too often, the people who are collectively giving millions of dollars to pay off a church's building won't give the same amount to help the people who live in the neighborhood where the church building is located.

I told Ms. Keeta that she was the true Holy Person because, according to Jesus, the people who clothed Him when

He was naked, fed Him when He was hungry, and visited Him when He was in prison, are the ones who will be called righteous when He returns. It is the ones like her who had mercy on their brother, forgave their brother, released the poor from their debts, loved the father, and loved His people. Even though Ms. Keeta is aware of her flaws, she is doing the work to minister unto Jesus.

The second part of what we must do said to "read the word of God daily." Why must we read the word of God daily? This is the advice given to us in the Bible. Joshua 1:8 says, "This book of the law shall not depart out of my mouth; but thou shalt meditate therein day and night, that thou mayest observe to do according to all that is written therein: for them thou shalt make thy way prosperous, and then thou shalt have good success."

How can reading the words in the bible prosper you? Does reading the words in any book change the circumstances of your outward life? Reading the Bible is different from reading the words of any other book because the words in the bible are alive. Jesus is the word of God. When you get his words in your spirit, your spirit is fed and nourished with truth. This allows Jesus to shine his light inside of you. Jesus can then work to produce the harvest in you. He will not give up on you.

Jesus will teach you how to forgive, love, give, whom to give to, how to develop your gifts and talents, and how to be successful. Jesus says that he can only do what the father sent Him to do. He was sent to save those who are lost. Our responsibility is to commune with Him (not by drinking wine and eating a dry piece of bread on 1st Sunday), but by obeying His words and speaking His words.

Rev 3:20 Behold, I stand at the door, and knock: if any man hear my voice, and open the door, I will come in to him, and will sup with him, and he with me. John 14:23 Jesus answered and said unto him, If an man love me, he will keep my words: and my Father will love him, and we will come unto him, and make our abode with him.

Circle which day of the week you will start to commit to reading/listening to the book of the law?

| Sunday | Monday | Tuesday | Wednesday | Thursday | Friday | Saturday |

Circle the time of day you can do it.

6	7	8	9	10	11	12	1	2	3	4	5
a m	a m	a m	a m	a m	a m	a m	a m	a m	a m	a m	a m
p m	p m	p m	p m	p m	p m	p m	p m	p m	p m	p m	p m

Circle the amount of time you will spend doing this.

minutes	hours
5 min	1 hr
10 min	2 hr
15 min	3 hr
20 min	4 hr
25 min	5 hr
30 min	6 hr
35 min	7 hr
40 min	8 hr
45 min	9 hr
50 min	10 hr
55 min	11 hr
60 min	12 hr

Create a measurable goal.

I will commit to listening to the book of the law on
_____ (day of week) at _____ (time of day) for
_____(minutes/hrs.).

Fast to Win the Fight

By Tamara Keeler

Invisible, though you may see
The enemy of you and me
Is working to oppose your dreams
And in your dreams you must believe

Let go of Fear, Let go of Doubt
Adultery you must cast it out,
Don't laugh or joke, they're not your friends
Watch what they do in the end

Sadness and Grief is not for you
Bitterness is not what we do
Happiness and Joy is meant for you
Live life to the fullness is what we do

The world is waiting to see your light
Restrict your intake and make the plight right
Break every evil covenant with all your might
Have Faith in Jesus and keep winning the fight

Chapter 2: Learn to Fast

Fasting will deliver you from EVERY enemy who opposes you. We are spiritual beings who can create the destiny we were meant to achieve. If there were no enemy opposing us, God's will in heaven would surely be done on earth. But I'm here to tell you that you are more than able to subdue your spiritual enemies through the power of fasting.

We learned that if we put our trust in man, our jobs, or a government program, we brought a curse upon ourselves. Now add one more item to that list…"food." That's right, putting our trust in "food" is also bad. In Matthew 4:4, Jesus is talking, and He says, "…Man shall not live by bread alone, but by every word that proceedeth out of the mouth of God." Food shouldn't be looked at as our provider.

Question for you. "If there were no food and no one to give you food, could you still eat?" Yes.

- God rained manna from heaven to feed the Children of Israel when there was no food in the desert.
- Jesus multiplied fish and a few loaves of bread to feed over four thousand people multiple times.
- Elijah ate cakes each day during the famine for over two years with one handful of meals. And before that, the birds brought him flesh to eat each day.

Philippians 4:19 says, "But my God shall supply all your need according to his riches in glory by Christ Jesus." These scriptures prove that there is no lack with God. Food does not determine whether we live or die, but God does. Therefore, in fasting, we purposefully afflict ourselves and place restrictions on the food that we eat to show our commitment and worship of the one who supplies our meals.

Discussion Question: Which is stronger: Our body or Our spirit?

Matthew 4:4 also reveals to us that our spirit has life because of the word of God. This means that our spirit needs to hear the word of God to stay strong and live. Proverbs 18:14 says, "The spirit of a man will sustain his infirmity; but a wounded spirit who can bear?" "Sustains his infirmity" means that your spirit can heal diseases in your body. Your spirit can sustain whatever injuries you have. However, the verse goes on to say that if your spirit is wounded, this does not work in reverse. This means that your body can't heal your spirit. Therefore, it says, "a wounded spirit who can bear." Your spirit is stronger than your body. It is important to feed and nourish your spirit by giving it the food that it eats: The Living Word of God.

I'm a living testimony of how this works. Years ago, I was suffering from depression and was taking prescribed medication that had all kinds of side effects, including nausea. And I was going to this church where each week the preacher would say, "You don't need depression medication. You need Jesus". I felt like he was speaking to me, but I ignored it. This preacher would say the same thing week after week. After the third week of hearing this same message, I listened to him and decided to stop taking my depression medication. Immediately, my symptoms came right back. I was not healed by faith, and I did not believe that pastor. Nevertheless, the Pastor preached the same message the next week, but I heard it differently this time. He said, "You don't need depression medication; you need to read the word of God and get Jesus." At that moment, I acknowledged that I had never read the word of God. I had only stopped taking the medication and had faith in my heart. I went home and started to read the book of Matthew. As soon as I finished reading the story of Jesus being tempted by the Devil after he had fasted and was hungered, I felt the spirit of depression as it was leaving my body. I was miraculously healed when my spirit heard the word of God.

What food did you eat today?

_____

What food did your spirit eat today?

_____

I feel invincible now that my spirit knows and believes the truth that I can truly create my path using my gifts. I can think bigger than the box people want to place me in and be accepted and successful because God accepts me, and my obedience to his word will make me successful. I heard Steve Harvey say that he knows a lot of people with education. They have degrees that they can't do anything with. But once you believe in your own gifts, education can support those goals and dreams. This is not just positive thinking. God's word will not return onto Him void. This is understanding how God has set up the earth to work with man having dominion and being fruitful in the system that was set up.

The lesson that you should understand with having dominion over everything that God created is that God is a spirit. His creation is alive, spiritual like Him, and is ruled by spirits. God is the God of spirits. For example, your dominion over water is dominion over living water and every spirit that rules water, including the spirit of frost, the spirit of the sea, the spirit of the clouds, the spirit of rain, the spirit of snow, the spirit of fog, the spirit of ice, the spirit of the river, etc. The commandment to subdue the earth means that we have authority in His name to calm a raging sea like Jesus did when he told the storm: Peace, be Still. (To learn more about the spiritual nature of the earth, please read the testimony of Enoch in the Book of Enoch: Gen 5:24; Heb 11:5; Jude 1:14.)

For example, in Joshua 10:12-13, the sun and moon obeyed Joshua when he commanded them to stand still. This means that the sun and moon are alive and are ruled by spirits. On the cloudy morning of my baptism, God encouraged me to pray for sunlight. All that morning and afternoon was overcast. As soon as I began to walk into the water, the clouds parted, and the light shone through for the duration of my baptism then closed again.

The prophet Isaiah prayed for the sun to move backward across the sky, and it was so, 2 Kings 20:11. Moses commanded the Red Sea to part so the Israelites could walk on dry ground. Jesus didn't wait for the water to part; He walked on top of the liquid water, even though we are taught to look at water and all liquids as dumb substances that are not alive.

Many things in the bible are spiritual and require faith in the word of God to produce an outcome. They require you to open your mind to new truths, even if those truths contradict what you were taught. God's truth will always trump our educational training and upbringing. For example, science may teach one thing, but God's truth may contradict science. God may respond to your pray with instructions for you to give clothing or a ride to someone in need. It may not make sense how your giving translates to your needs being met.

Personally, I have a logical process mindset. I also have a Bachelor of Science degree in engineering. In science we were taught that objects like stones and rocks are not alive. Britannica.com defines life as any system capable of performing functions such as eating, metabolizing, excreting, breathing, moving, growing, reproducing, and responding to external stimuli. This definition reinforces the belief that stones and rocks are not alive. However, the word of God indicates that stones are alive.

- Luke 19:40 says that stones will cry out to praise God if people don't.
- Hab 2:11 says that stones can cry out and beams of timber can give answer.

- Jacob made a heap of stones the witness between him and Laban in Genesis 31:48.
- Moses was prevented from seeing the promised land because he did not speak to the rock to command it to bring forth water in Numbers 20:8-12.

This means that a living spiritual component was present with the rock. The rock understood language and was capable of becoming a portal between a realm of powerful water and a realm of a dry wilderness. The rock delivered enough water to quench the thirst of 6 million people along with their livestock. Therefore, contrary to what science teaches, stones are alive and have a spiritual aspect that can serve as a witness to an agreement made by two people on earth.

Furthermore, the bible says that animals who can't speak our languages or testify in court can serve as witnesses to a contract.

- Abraham made seven ewe lambs the witness that he dug a well in Genesis 21:30.

This means that our possessions are spiritual and recorded in the spiritual realm. If any spirit steals something that belongs to us, we can petition God and call up our spiritual witnesses to verify our claim.

What are a few truths from the bible that contradict your logical education?

a. _____

b. _____

c. _____

Our fasting will break the spiritual bands of wickedness. You must also believe that there are people with spiritual chains around them, and they are not free. I was in bondage to the spirit of Anxiety. Even though I was walking around as free as could be, I was mentally broken. I could barely speak an entire sentence without taking two and three breaths between my words. I had major migraines and could not bow my head to pray. I could no longer drive a car, and I could feel the pressure of that spirit in my body every day for over six months. I couldn't work; I couldn't care for my children.

I knew that my answer was found in consistent fasting and prayer. However, fasting had not been possible for me during my pregnancy or breastfeeding stages. I needed to figure out a way to fast for the extended amount of time without affecting my newborn son. I decided that my fast would consist me eating only fruits and vegetables. I would eliminate eating out, take out, and store bought snacks. Basically, every aisle of the grocery store was off limits to me. No Grubhub or Doordash deliveries either. After 14 days of eating like this, I woke up one morning and felt normal. That spirit was gone.

Isaiah 58:5-7 says that the purpose of a fast is to loose the bands of wickedness, let the oppressed go free, undue heavy burdens, not hide from your flesh, & give to the hungry. Everything listed is spiritual, not physical. How can we see "bands of wickedness" around a person walking around free, not in prison? Jesus tried to explain it to the Pharisees, but they refused to set their mind on their spiritual bondage and only focused on their physical heritage. John 8:33-36 says, "They answered Him, We be Abraham's seed, and were never in bondage to any man: how sayest thou, Ye shall be made free?" (Jesus responds in truth and explains to them), "Verily, verily, I say unto you, Whosoever committeth sin is the servant of sin. And the servant abideth not in the house for ever: *but* the Son abideth ever. If the Son, therefore shall make you free, ye shall be free indeed."

Once again, we see that to sin is to serve the spirits of sin, which means that there are spirits who tempt us to lie, cheat, murder, restrict good from others, be angry, accuse our neighbor, not forgive, etc., all that we can become their slaves, in bondage to them. Why? Because they don't have any dominion on the earth except to get it from us. They want to exercise their will, their lust, and their wickedness. We are the gate keepers who stand in their way.

They try to trick us in our dreams to agree with their demonic ways. They plant false thoughts in our minds in order to tempt us to break God's commandments in our hearts. They try to play on our ignorance of how covenants with the world are forged, thereby making our authority over them null and void. They want to take up residence in our bodies and begin to cause trouble on the earth.

Name the evil spirits that are taking up residence in your life

The Spirit of _____

The Spirit of_____

The Spirit of_____

How would it benefit you if these spirits were removed?

If the Spirit of _____ was removed from my life_____.

If the Spirit of _____ was removed from my life_____.

If the Spirit of _____ was removed from my life_____.

When you worship in spirit, your spirit has authority over all evil spirits that are here, according to Genesis 1:28. It says, "And God blessed them, and God said unto them, Be fruitful, and multiply, and replenish the earth, and subdue it: and have dominion over the fish of the sea, and over the fowl of the air, **and over every living thing that moveth upon the earth.**"

Jesus says that as his disciples, we will do greater things than him. John 21:25 says, "And there are also many other things which Jesus did, the which, if they should be written every one, I suppose that even the world itself could not contain the books that should be written. Amen." Just like Jesus, you, too, have the authority and encouragement to subdue evil spirits who move on the earth. And just like Jesus, you, too, can cancel the sickness, disease, confusion, murder, poverty, death, grief, and chaos that they bring.

Jesus fasted for forty days and was able to subdue every evil spirit, including the wisest spirit, Satan. I'm going to give you the steps to fast that you can begin to see immediate results in your life and the lives of your loved ones. As you strengthen your spirit with the word of God and your faith in the power of God, the results of your fasting will become greater and greater until not even Satan can oppose you. But it starts with a commitment to begin.

The benefits of believers' fasting can be seen in the biblical story of the little boy who was possessed by a lunatic spirit. The disciples of Jesus did not fast while Jesus was with them, and they were not powerful enough to cast out the spirit that was causing the little boy to burn himself and drown himself. Matthew 17:19 and Mark 9:28 record the disciples asking Jesus why they couldn't cast him out. Jesus told them that only fasting and prayer could cast him out.

Here are the steps to fasting:

#1 Commit to Stop drinking or eating something
#2 Continue to Repent of your sins (Start at Exodus 20)
#3 Obey the Voice of God – Listen and obey what you hear
#4 Pray the scriptures that will break the bondage
#5 Praise God – It will bring God's blessings right to you
#6 Thank God for everything in faith that you are asking for
#7 Give to those in need – (A word, food, clothes, a ride, etc.)

Tamara, what's up with #1? Why can't I fast by stopping some activity that I enjoy, like watching the tv? If you can break spiritual bondage by stopping an enjoyable activity, then more power to you. I'm just a messenger here to tell you that God's word will not return unto Him void. According to the bible's examples of fasting (restricting something food &/or drink), you will get the results that scripture promises. I can't tell you the results of any other type of fast you choose to put your faith in. I will tell you that Satan likes to tempt God's people to eat from the tree of good and evil by corrupting the perfect word that God has already been spoken.

Furthermore, the Book of Enoch can give you some background information to understand why restricting food or drink is a beneficial weapon to overcome evil spirits versus fasting, an activity like watching tv. The book of Enoch explains that evil spirits were the children of women and the angels. These children grew into giants and acquired all of the acquisitions of men. When they died, their spirits were not allowed in heaven, because unlike man, they were created on the Earth. In their giant form, they were very fleshly, glutenous, always thirsty, and are never filled. They can only be granted power from the use of a person's body. Therefore, when we fast from food or drink and take our focus off of fleshly desires, it breaks any covenants we have with them in our bodies. It frees us from being controlled by their desires.

Create a measurable goal.

- I will commit to break the spiritual bands of wickedness brought about by the Spirit of _____(name of spirit) for _____ (length of time).

- I will believe the following scriptures that oppose this spirit:

  _____

  _____

  _____

- I will give to those in need while I fast by _____ (cooking a meal, giving clothing, feeding the hungry, sharing a positive message, etc.)

- I will continue to repent/forgive/confess/mend relationships/and renew my mind of negative thoughts while I fast.

- I will pay attention to my dreams and break any covenants I have made with my spiritual enemies.

Chapter 3: Fasting Doesn't Work For Me

"Tamara, I've done all those steps, and fasting just doesn't work for me." "God doesn't say anything to me when I fast." "I've fasted for 53 days in total last year, given to help people, and prayed for God to help me, but I'm still in the same situation." Really? So, you're telling me that God's word is a lie. You're telling yourself and me that God's word can return to Him void? Today the mystery will be revealed to you why Christians or people who love God fast incorrectly and then feel like God is a liar. Let God be true, and every man be a liar.

This idea of "I've fasted, and nothing happened" is so misunderstood that it's discussed at least three times in the Bible. The first example is in the book of Job talks about how Job felt like God was a big "meanie" who was not answering his prayers at a time when Job was sick with nothing left in life to live for. Job felt like God hated him and showed him no mercy. But it was revealed that the problem was with Job. Job never let go of his fear or his pride which allowed him to be the servant of sin. Job also ignored the revelation that he was shown in his dreams. We learned that there is nothing we can do, either good or bad, that affects God. Everything we do affects us. God is always loving and merciful that we can have the abundant life that He gave us.

The second example can be found in the book of Isaiah chapter 58 and Matthew chapter 11. The book of Isaiah tells us that the Israelites fasted unto God in ashes, with their heads bowed down and in prayer. They thought that this public display of humility was considered a fast. They accused God of not answering their prayers. But it was revealed that they were filled with the spirit of anger and revenge. Inwardly, they were not humbled at all. Their actions had nothing to do with the will of God or the character of God. God says that revenge belongs to Him alone. God says to show ourselves to be children of the kingdom of heaven by forgiving those who despitefully use us and praying for them. To have the audacity to judge God shows another sin, pride. Like Job, these people were filled with the Sprit of pride. They had the nerve to falsely accuse God of not doing his part, when God is the only one who delivers on his promise every time.

Jesus explains their actions in Matthew 11:16-19. He says that this generation is like children playing in a market. "We have piped to you, and you have not danced." "We have mourned unto you, and ye have not lamented." For John came not eating and drinking and was judged by the people. But Jesus came eating and drinking and was judged by the people. What's being revealed is that the people who expect God to dance to their tune, doesn't even like God. They are full of judgement of God and judgment of his servants.

We have demonstrated that on two separate occasions, the problem lies within the people who are fasting incorrectly. Yet, they are the ones falsely accusing God of not answering their prayers.

Humble Yourself

Try this exercise...it requires you to humble yourself and consider that there may be something you are missing or doing incorrectly. Ask yourself if you are someone who needs to be convinced that fasting does indeed work. If that statement is true for you, then it's likely that you skipped over writing down a fasting goal in the chapter one exercise. Do me a favor. After you read this chapter, go back to chapter one and write down a fasting goal. Please allow me to show you one way of examining yourself in order to learn where the problem may lie.

This is so important for me to help you because you are a shining light to many people whom you encounter. God wants you to be a blessing in their life and even show them that fasting does work. However, it will be difficult for you to testify about fasting if you haven't seen concrete results in your own life. It would be difficult for you to bless others if you have not used fasting in your own life to gain spiritual power.

I have seen concrete results in my life, time and time again. My life has gone from cursed to blessed through fasting many times. Deitrick Haddon & Voices of Unity has a song entitled "He's Able" with the following lyrics, "Don't give up on God, and he won't give up on you, he's able". I want to encourage you that Jesus is going to keep working to shine your light brighter and brighter. You can learn if you are doing anything wrong when you try to fast because Jesus says that there is nothing hidden that won't be revealed, Matthew 10:26.

Just think about how many more people you could bless and help if your spiritual enemies were overcome. Jesus healed thousands of people and cured every sickness, brought back the dead, restored limbs, and cured mental issues and chronic medical conditions. Let's focus on who you have come across who needs help? You are the light to bring the kingdom of God to them. You are the solution to their problem. You learning how to fast to get results, may be the difference between someone suffering and them being healed.

Who could you help or inspire if fasting really worked for you?

1. _____
   _____

2. _____
   _____

3. _____
   _____

4. _____
   _____

5. _____
   _____

6. _____
   _____
   _____

7. _____
   _____

8. _____
   _____

9. _____
   _____
   _____

Satan has the power to take your stuff if you agree with him. Amos 3:3 asks, "Can two walk together, except they be agreed?" Matthew 18:19-20 testifies that if two of you shall agree on earth as touching anything they ask, it shall be done for them of my Father, which is in heaven. This means that if a spirit like Satan comes into agreement with a man like Job, then whatever they agree on shall also come to pass. On the other hand, if a spirit like God comes into agreement with an obedient man like Abraham, then whatever they agree on shall come to pass as well.

Job was buddies with the Spirit of Fear. Job 3:25 says, "For the thing which I greatly feared is come upon me, and that which I was afraid of is come unto me." I thought the thing that we greatly feared was God. Fear was an idol to Job. Job broke the 1st of the 10 commandments by putting his fear before God. He became a slave to his sin and gave Satan permission to do what Satan does best: steal, kill, and destroy. Contrary to popular belief, there would have been no way for Satan to harm Job if the sin was not already present.

Why is this true when we can clearly read that God gave Satan permission to attack Job after he was declared an upright man? It is true because nowhere does God say that two spirits can come together to agree, and it shall be done. Spirits have to make covenants with man in order to have their will done on the Earth. The Spirit of God and the Spirit of Satan are no exceptions. When the Lord speaks with Satan in Job 1:12 to discuss Job, they were two spirits speaking with one another. Whatever they decide to do in heaven will still hinge on the authorization granted by Job to Satan's kingdom. We learned that God's word will never return unto Him void. God gave man dominion on Earth. It is up to every man to give the authority for any spirit to act out their will upon the Earth.

The best evidence to prove these statements is to demonstrate why we have the right to salvation and to a blessed life free from curses. It is the story of when this law was violated. It is the documented time when a spirit harmed a man without that man granting permission. It is the story of the death of our Messiah.

In Matthew 4:1-11 Satan was permitted to tempt Jesus after He had fasted for 40 days and was hungry. Jesus did not come into agreement with him but resisted all of Satan's temptations by using the word of God. Matthew 16:23 records where Satan used Peter to try to tempt Him into agreement. Jesus continued to resist Satan's temptations in His life. Matthew 26:36-46 tells the story of Jesus in the garden of Gethsemane where He prayed three times to overcome the sorrow of his soul, accepting God's will for His life in the end.

The entire reason we have been redeemed is because Satan continued with his attacks on a righteous man all the way until He died. This death of an innocent man who never broke a commandment of God marked the coming end to Satan's rulership on Earth. With that one violation of God's law, Satan lost the keys to death and total rulership over the Earth. A rulership that was originally given to Adam. Satan handed over those keys to Jesus, who has restored those keys to us. As we say, "Satan fumbled the bag," while Jesus "Secured the bag." Now we are not only redeemed to everlasting life, with no death, but we also have the authority to take back everything the enemy stole from us, NOW. We have the authority to heal all disease and sickness, NOW. We have the authority to claim every resource we need to produce a harvest on Earth as it is in Heaven, NOW. Jesus came that we can have an abundant life, and abundance is our portion, NOW.

Name something that Satan has killed, stolen, or destroyed in your life, that you need back NOW?

_____

In Isaiah 58, the Lord rebukes the fast that the children of Israel were doing. He asks them, "Is it such a fast that I have chosen?" Think about this question when it comes to the type of fast that you are doing. The people at that time were fasting outwardly in their appearance. The Lord informed them that the first thing required in a fast is to lose the bands of wickedness. This is to take the list that you wrote about all the people who could benefit from your fast and begin to break the bondages in your life and in theirs. We are to feed them, clothe them, house them, and encourage them. No one has to know that you are fasting, but they should see your giving, joy, and concern for them. If we do these simple things, God promises to let our light break forth as the morning, and our health shall spring forth speedily. It says our righteousness shall go before us, and the glory of the Lord shall be our reward.

Isaiah 58 spills over into chapter 59 with the Lord continuing his rebuke of their ungodly actions while fasting.

1. Have you brought up the forgiven sins of others?
2. Are you doing His will on the Sabbath?
3. Have you spoken against unrighteousness?
4. Are your hands defiled with blood?
5. Are your fingers full of iniquity?
6. Have your lips spoken lies?
7. Has your tongue muttered perverseness?
8. Are your thoughts of iniquity or accusations?
9. Are your thoughts of revenge?
10. Have you made peace with those who love you?

Righteousness is a bulletproof vest. Doing righteous acts offers spiritual protection. Isaiah 59:17 says, "For He put on righteousness as a breastplate..." But evil-doers have no breastplate because their actions are spider webs that "...shall not become garments..." Isaiah 59:6. This is why we need to learn what sin is in order to repent of it.

Start at Exodus 20:1-3. Read the scripture, then compare your life to what it says. We need to examine ourselves by looking at the law and seeing our reflection as if we were looking in a mirror. Next read Exodus 20:4-6, compare your life to what it says. Continue doing this exercise until you've gotten through all the commandments of God. I usually find all foundational laws of the bible in the first five books of the bible (Genesis, Exodus, Leviticus, Numbers, Deuteronomy), then Psalms, Proverbs, the four gospels of Jesus (Matthew, Mark, Luke, John), the book of Acts, (I John, II John, III John, James, Jude, Revelation).

How can one learn to perfect a new skill without having context as to what "good looks like"? If you want to learn how to take good pictures it might be a good idea to learn the quality standards for "What makes a good picture." For example, in the past whenever I snaped a photo of my daughter, "the unofficial photographer in our family" she would immediately disapprove of the picture. I had no clue why the photo that I enjoyed taking was all wrong. But she taught me how to understand a few quality standards for what makes a good photo. For family portraits, there should not be random people walking in the background or bad shadows on people's faces. For individual pictures using the portrait mode camera setting creates softer backgrounds and sharper focused subjects.

Learning the quality standards of how to live life from the bible is the same way. We have to read the standard from the bible, then look at our life to judge if it is meeting the standard or not. Sad to say, but it's educated Christian women, who were like me, that I usually have the hardest time ministering to. I was Christian woman who thought that I was living in the light. I thought that because I was studying to be a Sunday school teacher that my life was qualified to teach the truth. Unbeknown to me, I was a hypocrite living in darkness.

The world can often see how your heart is not right, hence the term "fake Christian" or "Christian Hypocrites". In order for you to see it for yourself you must compare your actions and your life to the standards found in scripture. Will you be brave and do it today? Can you read the truth of God without making excuses to justify your ways? Can you look into the mirror and see your true reflection?

When I looked into the mirror of God's truth, I did not like what I saw. There was no one who could have changed me or told me that I was a sinner on my way to hell. God's truth was staring me right in my face and I knew that my actions were causing me to agree to Satan. My actions and my thoughts were keeping me cursed. My mindset needed to be renewed according to God's truth.

Well, like me, the Israelites in Isaiah 58 thought that they were the holiest of the holiest. But the Lord took one look at them and read them all the ways they were unrighteous, according to his word. You see, Satan cannot cast out Satan. Unholiness can't fast against unholiness and get a result. Set a schedule for when you will read or listen to the laws of the bible then use the chart below to compare your life to what you read.

Bible Truth	Your Life

Chapter 4: Separate from your sins

The words you speak have the power to separate you from biblical sin, generational curses, spirits from your dreams, and covenants that you personally made. You can use your words to free yourself from every curse preventing you from living an abundant life. It starts with getting more knowledge about how spirits legally make covenants with you and obtain the right to curse you. It ends with you speaking the scriptures to repent & break the curse in Jesus's name.

Repentance is the spiritual separation from sin. Since he who sins, serves the spirit behind the sin, to speak repentance is to take back power and authority from the spirit you were serving and lift the curse. Therefore, repentance is you freeing yourself from spiritual prison, then becoming the warden with the authority of imprisoning the very spirits who enslaved you until they pay restitution back to you.

"If I'm already a Christian, what do I need to repent of?" For people who believe in cosigning & giving to wicked people, Proverbs 6:5 says, "Deliver thyself as a roe from the hand *of the hunter*, and as a bird from the hand of the fowler."

In Matthew 10:35, Jesus says, "For I am come to set a man at variance against his father, and the daughter against her mother, and the daughter in law against her mother-in-law." Jesus is speaking of a spiritual separation that needs to occur, to free his people. It requires us to repent from being in covenant with masquerading spirits who are familiar spirits who pretend to be our loved ones.

Leviticus 20:6 "And the soul that turneth after such as have familiar spirits, and after wizards, to go a whoring after them, I will even set my face against that soul and will cut him off from among his people." Many people get comfort from dreaming of their deceased parents, children, grandchildren, or pets. But do you know that these are masquerading spirits sent to cause you death, theft, poverty, and sickness? They may resemble your loved ones, but Jesus says that they are not of his kingdom and our covenants with them need to be broken to set us free from their curse.

God says to "put no other God before me." God says anyone who loves their father or mother more than Him is not worthy of Him. To accept a spirit in your dream who resembles a past loved one is to put that wicked spirit before Him. You must repent if you have done this. Repentance is Strong's number H7725, and it means "to be sorry" or "to comfort". H5162, also means to "breathe deeply" "to repent". It is comforting to hold our deceased loved one dear to our hearts. Some people swear that they can feel the presence of them. Take a breath and find the comfort in releasing your loved ones to God. Then accept God's provision for your life. Love the son, above your need to be comforted. Trust Him above your need to be right. Satan only comes to steal, kill, and destroy. Familiar spirits are of the kingdom of Satan. If they are with you, I guarantee that it is not for your good.

We learned from our discipleship mission that we are disciples of the Lord, and we are supposed to continue the work that he identified as his mission. But James 4:4 indicates that whosoever is a friend of the world is an enemy of God. Ouch! We're trying to bless people, and here we learn that all the people who we're in covenant with could be the reason why we are cursed and not blessed.

Yes, I learned that you could pray or fast for someone all you want. But if that person has not broken their covenants with the world, then their agreement with the world may supersede any intervention that you are attempting to help with. What has righteousness to do with unrighteousness? My family was once praying for a close relative to have favor granted to them by the court system. We even fasted and had many scripture quotes to get the desired outcome. But lo and behold, the favor was not granted. When I asked the Lord why not, He responded by indicating that His hands were tied. He said that there were covenants that were not broken with our close relatives and the world. I went to my relative and asked if what I heard from God was true. They confirmed that they agreed with the actions of worldly people, but had no idea that by doing so, they hindered their own prayers.

because there was no understanding that by them agreeing with worldly people's actions, they were coming under the same judgment of those people and hindering their own prayers.

The world may love and accept everyone and strive for world peace, but the truth is that the bible teaches spiritual separation. PERIOD.

- Matthew 5:17 Jesus says, "Think not that I am come to destroy the law, or the prophets: I am not come to destroy, but to fulfill." **He came for those who will obey Him.**

- Matthew 9:13 "...I will have mercy, and not sacrifice: for I am not come to call the righteous, but sinners to repentance. **He came for those who will have mercy.**

- Matthew 10:34-36 "Think not that I am come to send peace on earth: I came not to send peace, but a sword..... And a man's foes shall be they of his household. **He came for those who would choose Him over their family.**

But once again, we need revelation knowledge to look deeper. God is a spirit, and we must worship Him in spirit. How does separating from people, who are flesh, help us to serve God, who is a spirit? The hidden truth is that the separation that He came to create is spiritual separation. Hebrews 4:12 says, "For the word of God is living and active and sharper than any double-edge sword, piercing even to the point of dividing soul from spirit, and joints from marrow: it is able to judge the desires and thoughts of the heart." Jesus is the word of God. He has come to bring sinners to repentance. Let's try to process what this means. When Jesus says that He came to deliver the captives, we learn that it was not a physical deliverance that was needed but rather a spiritual one.

If I was enjoying lustful actions before I repented, that means that I was a slave to the Spirit of Lust. I was serving that Spirit and allowing it to rule over me. The moment I have a change of heart and confess and repent of my sins, speaking in the name of Jesus, the living word of God, that two-edge sword divides the Spirit of Lust from your joints and marrow. Let me tell you all that happened. My mother passed on ten years ago. But I would often see her in my dreams. This was not my mother but a masquerading spirit pretending to be her. There were generational curses in my bloodline that needed to be broken. The curses from my mother's side of the family were trying to continue to steal and rob me. I could have decided to love my mother and desire to see her in my dreams, or take a stance and love Jesus by either rebuking the masquerading spirit in the dreams, or after I awoke. I had enough spiritual insight to rebuke the spirit in my dream and after I awoke from the dream.

Jesus said that He came to cause spiritual division. Telling people to rebuke their deceased loved ones in dreams can cause division in families. Anyone who is truly obeying the bible will have trouble in his home because shifting our physical actions will cause trouble with our spiritual enemies. When I was just living a regular Christian life, going to church on Sundays and paying tithes, I had no trouble in my home. But when I changed to obey the commandments, my family was mad at me and wanted to disown me. Tell your kids that you are not celebrating Christmas anymore. Or tell your husband that "this is an idol or that is an idol," and you want to make some changes in your life…watch the division begin to occur. Change the way you dress to start wearing fringes on your clothing; people will call you crazy or rebel against you. That is what happed to me.

I told my family that I wanted to add the Passover Holy Day to keep it and purchase a tent to live in it for a week to celebrate the Feast of Tabernacles. I had a fight on my hands. After I stopped eating the unclean food of pork, one person in my family purposely mixed bacon into the food they prepared for me and tried to act like they had no idea where the bacon came from or how it got on my sandwich. I found the bacon carefully hidden in the back of the fridge. God's laws are very simple to follow, and their hidden meaning is all about loving Him and loving one another. But our spiritual enemies will rise within our loved ones to oppose us with these small changes that will help you go from a cursed to a blessed life.

Living a blessed life is living according to a higher standard. God told the children of Israel that he did not put them in the promised land because of their righteousness but rather because of the wickedness of the people who were living there. The Israelites' were forbidden to do the same things that the people before them did, less they would suffer the same judgements that those people suffered. God said that his laws are what separated the Children of Israel from the people who lived in the land of Canaan. As soon as the Children of Israel broke his laws, his judgments were activated and they too got kicked off the land or they had their enemies overcome them.

Chapter 5: Don't Defile Yourself

You can be defiled if you accept the misguided words of your teachers. Matthew 16:6-12 says,

> "Then Jesus said unto them, Take heed and beware of the leaven of the Pharisees and of the Sadducees." " ..." "How is it that ye do not understand that I spake it not to you concerning bread, that ye should beware of the leaven of the Pharisees and of the Sadducees? Then understood they how that he bade them not beware of the leaven of bread, but of the doctrine of the Pharisees and of the Sadducees?"

This reveals to us that when our Lord is speaking about the bread, He is speaking about accepting the misguided words that were coming out of the mouth of someone. The Pharisees taught that if you have something to give, and two choices on where to give it (either to the temple or to a godly person in need), you are free to ignore God's commandment of giving it to the person.

In the garden of Eden, Eve accepted the misguided words that she received from the serpent. She ate from the tree of Good and Evil first in her mind, then her actions followed. You are not to follow people who speak the words of the bible and then do the opposite. This is the exact reason why I stopped attending church. I was trying to hang on if possible. I kept attending the Wednesday night bible study. The last straw for me was when I heard them teach a beautiful lesson about the Holy Day of Passover and they twisted the message at the end.

The teachers went through the history of Passover and its purpose. They even had maps of the route that the children of Israel walked from Egypt to the Red Sea. At the end of the lesson, they said, "And this is why we keep communion today."

I was like, "huh?" I didn't read anywhere that God commanded the Feast of the Passover to end, go away, stop, or be replaced by Communion. "Hello! Can anyone hear me?" No one would give me an answer of why they were sticking to tradition and not still celebrating the Passover. The only answer I received was, "Well, the Jews still keep the Passover." Yes, and I'm a biblical Jew. But like the Pharisees, this group of believers were holding on to the traditions of man. They referenced biblical lessons but ignored truth of the scripture. Do not accept misguided words when the truth is staring you in the face.

Jesus is the true bread which came down from heaven. If we eat His flesh and drink His blood, we will live forever, John 6:58. If we follow His commandments and obey His teachings, we shall have everlasting life. We commune with Him when we obey His word. He is a spirit who speaks to our minds and our hearts. Rev 3:20 says, "Behold, I stand at the door and knock: if any man hear my voice, and open the door, I will come in to him, and will sup with him, and he with me."

Eve listened to the serpent's twisted words, then Adam followed Eve's actions, which allowed death to be passed on to all of us. Revelation 2:23 says, "And I will kill her children with death; and all the churches shall know that I am He which searcheth the reins and hearts: and I will give unto every one of you according to your works." Death was passed on to all of us who come from Adam. It remains the reward of people who choose to continue to listen to half-truths from people who preach the word but then follow man's tradition.

In Matthew 23:23, Jesus cursed the Pharisees and Scribes, saying that they pay tithe of mint, anise, and cummin but leave out things like law, mercy, judgment, and faith. I've learned that true judgment is showing mercy to others according to how we would like to be judged in mercy. It's forgiving people who owe you money when you know that they just can't afford to pay. It's helping strangers, widows, and their children because God loves these groups of people very much. It's having faith in God and knowing that He is your provider, even when a man can't or won't pay you back or help you out.

We must stay focused on the rule or the commandment versus the consequences. Satan comes to us with deception and confusion to trick us into agreeing with him. One tactic he uses is to get us to focus on the consequences instead of the rule. For example, Eve knew the rule that she was not permitted to eat from the tree of Good & Evil. But Satan changed her focus to look on the consequences saying, "Ye shall not surely die." Once we take our eyes off of the commandment of God to focus on whether or not we would get caught, get severely punished, or get any reprimanding, then we position ourselves to become slaves to sin.

What are some common sayings opposite the truth found in scripture?

	Worldly saying	Truth in Scripture
1	It's better to ask for forgiveness than permission.	The blessing of the Lord is without sorrow. You'll have nothing to be sorry for afterward.
2	It's better to weigh the consequences of your actions before making a decision.	Obey the commandment regardless of what you think you might get away with.

3	You can have fear and faith.	God did not give us the spirit of fear. You cannot serve God and mammon.
4		
5		
6		
7		
8		
9		
10		

Satan and his kingdom stays focused on the lust of the flesh, the lust of the eyes, and the pride of life. We can see all three of these things in the transaction between Eve and the serpent. The lust of the flesh was her desire to be wise. The lust of the eye was her seeing that the fruit was good for food. The pride of life was her thinking that she could be like God and be more than what he created her to be. The trade she made led to her death. If we weigh our actions and common beliefs against the commandments of God versus looking at the consequences or our fleshly desires, then we will do well to make good choices that bless our lives versus curse our lives.

You can be defiled from the food you are eating. I debated with myself whether or not to add this section on proving that you are to be separate from ideas and people who do not follow and obey God, but you should also be separate from certain foods such as pork, catfish, and crab legs.

I debated with myself because I now understand that it is more important to eat the truth, the true word of God, versus not eating pork.

God judges the hearts, and He has many servants who love Him and are cheerful givers, but those servants may also eat many foods that you are not supposed to eat. God has an abundance of grace for our ignorance of sin, as evident in laws that start with words like, "When a man learns that he has sinned, or when a king learns that he has sinned, or when the congregation learns that they have sinned." God only requires repentance for things when we become aware that we did something wrong.

Nevertheless, even the child Daniel knew that if he ate the "king's meat," it would defile him, Daniel 1:8. New believers should also know that God has a reason for why He instructed us not to consider animals like swine as food. Personally, when I stopped eating animals that the bible restricts, I lost more weight and improved my ability to hear from God. I gained an understanding of how to hear Him better in dreams, and I could see and understand the attacks against me in dreams from spiritual enemies. I felt like it was because my temple was not so polluted with unclean foods.

I do not profess to know why God has instructed us to do any of his commandments; accept that He has promised to move us from being cursed to blessed. So, here goes a bible study lesson on food restrictions.

The laws given to man for what he can eat have gone from being very restricted of fruit and herbs with seeds to including all green things and meats of animals. Genesis 9:3 says, "Every moving thing that liveth shall be meat for you; even as the green herb have I given you all things." But this statement has restrictions including the fact that eating blood is restricted. We'll learn in the book of Leviticus that anything that was a bottom feeder animal or unclean is still not allowed among the food selections of man.

Leviticus 11:1-9 contains dietary food laws for beasts.

- Whatsoever parteth the hoof and is clovenfooted, and cheweth the cud, among the beasts, that shall ye eat
- The camel is unclean unto you
- The coney is unclean unto you
- The hare is unclean unto you
- The swine is unclean unto you
- Of their flesh shall you not eat, and their carcass shall you not touch

Leviticus 11:10-12 contains dietary food laws for fish

- And all that have not fins and scales in the seas, and in the rivers, of all that moves in the waters, and of any living thing which is in the waters, they shall be an abomination unto you:

Leviticus 11:13-20 contains dietary food laws for fowl

- And these are they which ye shall have in abomination among fowls; they shall not be eaten, they are an abomination: the eagle and the ossifrage, and the ospray,
- The vulture and the kite are unclean
- The raven is unclean
- The owl, night hawk, cuckow, and hawk are unclean
- The little owl, cormorant, and great owl are unclean
- The swan, pelican, and gier eagle are unclean
- The stork, heron, lapwing, and bat are unclean

- All fowls that creep, going upon all four, shall be an abomination unto you

Leviticus 11:21-22 contains dietary food laws for creeping things

- Yet these may you eat of every flying creeping thing that goeth upon all four, which have legs above their feet, to leap withal upon the earth;
- The locust is ok
- The bald locus is ok
- The beetle is ok
- The grasshopper is ok
- But all other flying creeping things, which have four feet, shall be an abomination unto you

Leviticus 11:29 contains dietary laws for things that creep upon the earth.

- These shall be unclean unto you among the creeping things that creep upon the earth; the weasel, and the mouse, and the tortoise after his kind,
- The ferret is unclean
- The chameleon is unclean
- The lizard is unclean
- The snail is unclean
- The mole is unclean
- Whatsoever goeth upon the belly, and whatsoever goeth upon all four, or whatsoever hath more feet among all creeping things that creep upon the earth, them ye shall not eat; for they are an abomination.

Let's explain why God said that we could eat everything that moves, but there are still restrictions to only animals that chew the cud and are cloven-footed or, in other words, "clean animals" that move. Let's start by asking ourselves this question: Did Noah and his sons know the difference between clean and unclean? Our answer can be found in Genesis 7:2-3, "Of every clean beast thou shalt take to thee by sevens, the male and his female: and of beasts that *are* not clean by two, the male and his female. Of fowls also of the air by sevens, the male and the female; to keep seed alive upon the face of all the earth." Noah and his sons knew the difference between clean and unclean beasts.

Furthermore, we can read in Genesis 8:20 that Noah knew to choose only a clean beast to sacrifice on his altar to the Lord. Even Cain and Abel knew the laws of God, as demonstrated in Genesis 4:4 when Abel brought the firstlings of his flocks, but Cain was disciplined for his inappropriate offering of the inferior fruit of the ground.

Here's another question for us to ask ourselves. Is God's word only in the books of Moses? No. God is alive, and he is a spirit who can speak to you right where you are. Since the beginning, he's been speaking his word, and he will continue to speak his word today. Many of the servants of God have never opened a Bible. Servants like King Cyrus, who God blessed even though Cyrus didn't know Him. But the truth of what is written has been spoken to them personally by the one who wrote it, because Jesus is alive.

Just to be thorough, let's check if anyone else before Leviticus 11 knew the difference between clean and unclean animals to eat. You want to understand if the people were on a restriction before Moses wrote it down in the book of Leviticus or not. Here are all the examples of people eating animals before the book of Leviticus.

- Genesis 18:6-8 Abraham made a calf, butter, milk
- Genesis 27:3-4 Isaac instructed Esau to make venison
- Genesis 27:9-10 Rebecca requests goats to make meat
- Exodus 12:5-10 Eat the lamb/goat for the Passover
- Exodus 16:4 Bread will rain from heaven
- Exodus 16:12-16 Quails and manna will be eaten

- Exodus 29:32 Aaron & his sons shall eat the flesh of a ram

In none of those examples did people eat anything unclean. Just like Noah, they knew the difference between righteousness and unrighteousness and clean and unclean. Therefore, when God says that he gives us everything that moves, he was speaking about the clean animals, as Moses clarified later when he wrote it down. This is similar to when God told Noah to take two of every animal into the ark, but later we saw that the clean animals went in seven by seven. And after that ark landed, Noah sacrificed some of the clean birds and animals as an offering to God.

Understand that today your body is the temple of the Holy Spirit. Our hearts and our minds are the altars of sacrifice to the Lord. Will you bless unclean food in the name of the Lord and eat it with your mouth? Or will you speak words that curse your own life (I'm broke, I don't have a job, I'm poor) and accept these thoughts in your mind? As I learned the deeper meaning of the commandments and broke away from our traditions of eating unclean things and thinking unclean thoughts, I began to hear from God clearer, and my life improved.

Chapter 6: Let Go of Your Fears

Money controls many of our decisions in life. How many kids we will have, when we get married, or which cupcake we will purchase all are influenced by Money. This is the opposite of God's economy. God gave man dominion, which means that you are the one who decides what needs to happen. Money and everything else on earth must obey you.

"Money is like an iron ring we put through our nose. It is now leading us around wherever it wants. We just forgot that we are the ones who designed it." Mark Kinney

Consider the following categories. Write down any examples of when you changed your original decisions based on money:

Health

_____

_____

Spirituality

_____

_____

Education / Personal Development

_____

_____

Business

_____

_____

Family Time

_____

_____

Animals

_____

_____

Mental/Emotional

_____

_____

Marriage/Relationship

_____

_____

Food

_____

_____

Children

_____

_____

Travel Plans

_____

_____

The spirit behind money gets a lot of worship. The fear of losing money is a form of idol worship. The drive to obtain money, the comfort of having enough money, the pride of achieving money, and the hurt of not having money are all forms of worship. The story of Nabal shows us how a curse comes on people who refuse to share what they have with the poor. "He that despiseth his neighbor sinneth: but he that hath mercy on the poor, happy is he." Proverbs 14:21

God's economy is not based on money. As the scripture alludes, it is based on giving to the poor. The spirit of happiness comes to those who give to the poor of God's kingdom. But those who sin are slaves to the spirit of their sin. This means that when Nabal chose not to give, he was serving a spirit of pride or rebellion or greed, but not the spirit of the Most High God.

Serving these other spirits placed him under a curse, and his reward was the spirit of bitterness and death.

When I was going to church and paying tithes, there was nothing left to give to help people in my neighborhood who had a need. I often turned my back on my flesh that I could give to the church. I received no blessing from doing these things, just more bills, more debt, and more confusion on why it seems like God turned his back on helping me progress. I worked a second job, drove all over the place, and took away even more time from my kids.

Proverbs 13:23 says that "Much food *is in* the tillage of the poor: but there is *that is* destroyed for want of judgment." Having more money is not the problem. According to biblical principles, managing the resources that we have and not creating a wise plan for wealth is usually where the issues lie. God taught me to have a budget. After working on that budget, I learned that I had enough money to pay my bills. Before my budget, I argued with people over money, and I dreaded paying bills each month. I remember being stressed out whenever my husband would hit the gas too hard while driving the car. I hated when people didn't pay me back the money that they promised to pay. I was a slave to money. It was my idol, and I needed to be set free.

You can let go of any fears and be who you were meant to be. Money is paper, made by man, and has no value other than the spiritual value you place on it. If you focus on having money, you focus on the "How" to get things done. But remember to be like the screenwriter and keep your focus on the "what" and "why." When you speak the things that you need, God may bring you money to meet your need or not. Several believers testify that free cars were delivered to them, houses were given to them, or clothing and food were dropped off to them. Believers have gotten blessings in the mail; grants, memberships, tickets, flights, etc. If your need is met, it doesn't matter if paper money was used. The point is that God will miraculously meet your need when you release your fear and trust Him to be your provider. To further prove this point, think about all the things you have done to help people that didn't involve money.

List a few things other than money that you have given to meet the needs of someone:

_____

_____

_____

_____

_____

Just like you have given to others to meet their needs, your need could be met without money being involved. Man uses money to assign value to things, but God places value in the people of his kingdom, the poor of the earth. Jesus says that when he returns, he will separate the righteous sheep from the unrighteous goats. The righteous were the ones who fed him, clothed him, and visited him in prison. It was revealed the unrighteous goats were the people who did not help the poor of the kingdom of God.

I have given offerings of sliced watermelon to the poor and received mental healing for my family. I've seen people who were unemployed receive a job offer when as little as $10 was given to help others in need. Everything multiplies when it's blessed and put into God's kingdom. Things are not given from heaven by the money value they hold, they are awarded based on the righteous covering of the asker. Jesus is the most righteous name to ask anything in.

Having a project with Him means that you have access to everything needed for that project. When two or more people come together to ask, you shall have whatsoever you ask. If this book is about you going from cursed to blessed, why does it take two or more people? Because being who you were meant to be is all about helping others to be better. Your project will bless the lives of others, right? Find one or two people to help and pray together about the things needed to break the bonds of wickedness off their lives. Enable them to let their light shine bright.

When you have a righteous mindset, asking for things like a light bill to be paid is the same as asking for a car. They have the same value because the name of your savior is priceless. It's up to you to determine how much faith you will have to receive it and how committed you are to being a good steward of the opportunities that come back to you.

For example, if you are thousands of dollars in debt and you decide to make an offering of what you have to the poor, a job offer may return to you. Take the job offer and use the money to pay off your debt. If an idea for a new venture returns to you, put the idea into action and have faith that it will prosper. If someone brings valuable items to you that you don't have a use for, accept the items and sell them to pay off your debt.

You can be confident that everything you need will be provided for you. Remember to be like the screenwriter and keep your focus on the "what" and "why." Remove any focus on the money or "people needed" aspect of it. For example, if you depend on a lawyer to help you with a legal matter, your focus is on the "how." A lawyer may be able to help you, but God can change the laws today and make your entire situation null and void. Remember not to make a man or a government program your hope.

Anyone who believes that they must work two or three jobs to provide for themselves likely sees money as their deliverer and has made it an idol. The truth is that God's word says that he wants us to work less, not more. He wants us to rest each week on His Sabbath days and rejoice in his promise to give us a final rest when He returns to conquer death. Matthew 11:28-30 says, "Come unto me all ye that labour and are heavy laden, and I will give you rest. Take my yoke upon you and learn of me; for I am meek and lowly in heart, and ye shall find rest unto your souls. For my yoke is easy and my burden is light." God's law doesn't even allow Israelite kings to multiply horses to themselves. This keeps the kings' dependence on Him as their protector and provider. God's economy is all about us giving to the poor and letting the light in us shine in the darkness to have no lack in our homes.

Chapter 7: Let Go of Your Deliverer

Typically, when the bible mentions idols, it is speaking about statutes that were built or groves that were planted by man. People worship these man-made things by bowing down to them or leaving an offering in front of them. Now, you will learn the deeper meaning of idol worship and understand how people stay cursed with excuses to hold on to their idols.

Idols can also be intangible. A good example of intangible idolatry is the "need to be respected." People have killed others because they felt disrespected. Truly, they worship spirits, like Leviathan, the water spirit, who is a king over all the children of pride, Job 41:34. Idols are spirits who live in people in drive them to think and do everything. Many people are mentally enslaved to these spirits, and they feel like they have no choice in the matter.

Pick a movie, any movie, and you will understand what Hollywood already knows. Every story starts with a vision that drives a person to do everything that they do. In every movie, that vision is the worship of either the Most High God or an idol spirit. Often times it is the spirit of money. The movie can be about a man who decides to rob a bank or work hard in school to get money. In both examples, the spirt of money is in control.

Sometimes the movie is about a man who wants to clear his name because his idol was his name. This is the case with the movie entitled Chinatown. The protagonist, Jake Gittes, was driven to trespass, steal records, and be violent to a woman all to clear his name. The value of having a good name meant everything to him.

But even Jesus was called Beelzebub, who is the king of the devils. Jesus was not driven to defend Himself or clear His name. Instead, Jesus taught that a servant is not better than his master. We should not be so offended when people tarnish our name. The Lord is our defender, and He will elevate us in the presence of our enemies. Your story starts with the vision of who God made you to be. Your drive is then doing everything possible to achieve that vision while letting your light shine in the lives of everyone you meet.

Idol worship is also being done whenever you substitute God with anything else that drives you or delivers you. Money, lying, drugs, thrill-seeking, and sleep are examples of things people substitute God for to deliver them.

People lie to save themselves and prevent themselves from getting caught. They lie to hurt others or deceive others from seeing the truth. They lie to make themselves look good or to get ahead. But to lie is to serve a lying spirit. God hates liars. Jesus often said, "I tell you the truth." And Revelation 21:8 says, "...all liars, shall have their part in the lake which burneth with fire and brimstone..." God's law requires truthfulness in business. "A false balance *is* abomination to the LORD: but a just weight *is* his delight." Proverbs 11:1.

People use drugs to escape their lives, pain, and past, or just to feel alive and be delivered from the day-to-day boredom. But Proverbs 31:5 indicates that drinking causes one to forget the law and pervert the judgment of any of the afflicted. I learned that we are disciples of Christ, and we have a job to do. We are to speak up for the stranger, the fatherless, the widow, and any who are afflicted. We are the judges of the Earth with dominion to subdue it. We are to let our light shine and heal the broken-hearted and preach the gospel to the poor. How can one do their duties as a disciple if they are serving spirits of drunkenness and drugs? Their loyalty is to their flesh and not the things of God.

Thrill-seekers and people who sleep all day fall into these same categories of idol worship by needing to be delivered by things external to God. If one sleeps all day, seek to be delivered from facing the day instead of focusing on all the goodness God had brought. There is no giving, preaching, sharing, just sleep. No spending time with their loved ones, no praying for others, or doing what God has purposed for them. They are putting sleep before God. It is an idol. Proverbs 26:16 says, "The sluggard is wiser in his conceit than seven men that can render a reason." These people are full of pride and will not be convinced that they are doing anything wrong by checking out of life. But we are commanded to "Let your light so shine before men that they may see your good works and glorify our Father in heaven." Matthew 5:16

The next set of people who practice idol worship hold on tight to their god. They are the people who have a need to be respected, in control, valued, loved, right, comforted, have a good reputation, and last but not least, the need to be accepted. Jesus says, "It is enough for the disciple that he be as his master, and the servant as his lord." Matthew 10:25

Why the need to feel respected all the time? Jesus is Lord of all, and they disrespected Him, beat Him, and hung Him on a tree. We are not better than Jesus. Why continue to serve that spirit of rejection and make it an idol? Think about the number of people in jail because they felt disrespected? "Someone stepped on my toe!" "Someone blew their horn at me in traffic." "Someone looked at my girlfriend the wrong way." "Someone told me my ideas were all bad." Many of these issues are petty and not worth getting angry or fighting over. However, the spirit of anger and rejection gets involved to stir the pot. The bible says that anger rests in the bosom of a fool. Jesus said that blessed are the merciful, for they shall obtain mercy. We are to pray for our enemies because truly, they unknowingly bless us when they come against us.

Let's talk about people who need to be loved or valued so much that when they don't get it, they act contrary to the word of God. People have killed out of revenge for not being loved. But God says that vengeance and recompense belong to Him, Deuteronomy 32:35. People have committed suicide for believing the lie that they are not loved, but God's truth is that he will never leave you nor forsake you. God doesn't withhold any good gift from his children. We are loved by Him with all power to heal the sick, bind evil spirits, and bring about his kingdom on Earth. But to idolize being loved by someone or being acknowledged by someone is to serve another God. Especially when this need leads one to do some of the other things that we have discussed, such as lie, sleep, or take drugs. Our actions, if done unto God in secret, will be rewarded openly by Him. To look for a public reward by some person is a trick of the enemy to rob you of a better blessing. But choosing love as your deliverer instead of God Almighty is what makes it an idol.

Question for you reader. Are you living a comfortable life? Are you willing to give it up if required? Just like Abraham was willing to love and trust God more than his need to protect his son, we are required to put God before all things, including our comfort, our false security, friends, lifestyle, and even our health. In the story of Job, a man tremendously blessed with wealth, he loved God with all his heart. But the Devil saw pride in Job and knew that he was not as perfect as he seemed to be.

God allowed all of Job's possessions, his children, his property, his wealth, and later his health to be taken away, but after all of this, Job did not recognize his sin nor repent of his sin. Job was sorrowful and did not understand why God was so mean to him. If we truly believe that God is a good God who will never leave us nor forsake us, we could build our faith and not put our comfort or discomfort before Him as an idol to gain temporary deliverance.

Romans 8:35-39 says, "Who shall separate us from the love of Christ? *shall* tribulation, or distress, or persecution, or famine, or nakedness, or peril, or sword? As it is written, For thy sake, we are killed all the day long; we are accounted as sheep for the slaughter. Nay, in all these things, we are more than conquerors through Him that loved us, for I am persuaded that neither death, nor life, nor angels, nor principalities nor powers, nor things present, nor things to come, nor height, nor depth, nor any other creature, shall be able to separate us from the love of God, which is in Christ Jesus our Lord."

Let's talk about acceptance. How far will you go to be accepted? Some kids have shot up an entire school for not being accepted. Rejection does hurt. But the need to feel acceptance should in no way be placed above God being our deliverer. Some people feel that if they are in the "in crowd," they are protected. As we discussed previously, they use that acceptance as their protection, such as being a part of a sorority or private club that wears the right colors or symbols or being a cop or just sitting with the cool kids at lunch. But Jesus said He came to divide and not bring peace. The only team is his team, his truth, his will, versus the world. For the first time, we publicly see cops breaking their code of silence to speak up for what is right. If we're on God's team, we are going to respect our sisters and brothers and not focus on whether or not we are accepted by our group. If you believe that being in the right group will get you all the connections and deliver you, then it has become your God and is a form of idol worship.

The first of the ten commandments says that God delivered you out of bondage in Egypt and to put no other Gods before Him. The second commandment says not to make any graven images of anything to worship. Obeying these commandments brings a blessing to your third and fourth generations. Disobeying these commandments bring a curse to your third and fourth generations.

The Israelites who were delivered from Egypt disobeyed these commandments. They wanted to go back to Egypt. They missed the leaks and the garlic and forgot about the bondage and how the Egyptians killed their male children. They had no mercy for their dead babies. They held no righteous judgment in their hearts. They didn't consider that God was righteous and wanted them to have their land where they would raise righteous children to be the light of the world.

The Lord told Moses, "Go, get thee down; for thy people, which thou broughtest out of the land of Egypt, have corrupted themselves: They have turned aside quickly out of the way which I commanded them: they have made them a molten calf, and have worshipped it, and have sacrificed thereunto, and said, These be thy gods, O Israel, which have brought thee up out of the land of Egypt." Exodus 32:8. Then the Lord said, "...let me alone, that my wrath may wax hot against them, and that I may consume them: and I will make of thee a great nation." Exodus 32:10

God was not very happy with what the people did. And I want to point out one thing that happened with this scenario. These events happened after they were delivered from Egypt after they saw all the blessings of God. This generation of

Israelites did not know God. They heard about Him from their fathers, but they did not know Him. Because they lived in Egypt, what did they do? They took on the customs of the Egyptians. They dressed like the Egyptians; they worshiped the same God as the Egyptians. The Isrealites even married the Egyptians. (We know that because when they came out of Egypt, there was a mixed multitude and the incident of the man who cursed God...his mother was an Israelite and his father, an Egyptian.) They Isrealites ate the food that the Egyptians ate. But God started to change all of that.

Question to you, reader: Has God delivered during a time when you were ignorant about Him and blessed you? Did He prevent you from mingling with the people who were around you? Did He stopped you from participating in the customs and traditions of the area you grew up with? We know that we are still in captivity, and this land in America is not our land in Caanan. But I'm asking if God has freed you from your ignorance and brought you mentally out of your captivity? Has He taken you from being homeless and given you a place to stay? Has He blessed your health? Has He granted you a job or answered your prayers? Has He delivered you from whatever was oppressing you or whoever was oppressing you to change your lifestyle? And yet we go back to what He delivered us from. Is that you today?

Because that's exactly what Israel did, they went back to worshipping this calf, and they called it God. We try to make all kinds of excuses for why we're going to hang on to that sinful stuff that was in our past. They called it God.

What I see happening today is people doing seemingly innocent demonic activities labeled as God. For example, Christians will celebrate Halloween, which is not of God, and they'll call it a Hallelujah party. But they are still giving reverence to that Spirit behind the holiday, in his season. Who told you to cover your face with a demonic mask to shun away evil? God gave man his image to have dominion over the earth. You are already the authority over evil spirits because you were made in the image of God and given dominion over the earth. It's like the serpent making Eve feel like she could be like God when she was already like God, living eternal life.

Christians will celebrate Christmas, put a tree in their house, which is an idol, and offer gifts at the base of the tree, which are sacrifices and gifts to this idol, and they'll call it God's birthday. They say, "Oh, we're giving honor to God." No, you are not giving honor to God when you practice this custom.

The same concepts apply to people in secret societies, fraternities, and sororities who have made covenants with evil alters. But, they say that when they go and volunteer or help children, they are doing it unto God. No, you're not doing it unto the Most High God. You are doing the same thing the Israelites did when they worshipped the golden calf and called it "the God that delivered us out of Egypt." You're not worshipping God, and God is not pleased.

My background is in the motorcycle world and street gangs where people will die for their "colors." People will honor their colors. They will choose to honor, help, and respect a person who was in their group versus someone who was not. That is a respecter of persons. That is not of God. God is not a respecter of persons. You are bound by these societies, private clubs, and organizations that you are bowing down to and worship, honoring and dying for. And just like God was angry with those Israelites and said He would consume them, you are a target of destruction for idol worship.

The same thing can be said if you worship your country's Flag. Standing to a flag, a tangible object made in a factory, and saluting it, is saluting the spirit behind the flag. I've seen people condemn anyone who doesn't stand to it or state that they will die for it. Rahab didn't abide by this rule. She stood with Israel on the side of God when her nation was about to be attacked.

Many die-hard sports fans idolized the symbol of their favorite team. They spend money for tickets but won't give a dime to help the homeless person who stands outside of the stadium in need.

God sent Moses to tell them how much He loved them and wanted to free them from oppression. Aaron and Moses did miracles in Egypt to show the people who God was and how powerful He was to free them. All the plagues that affected the Egyptians: the plague of locusts, flies, blood, etc., none of them affected the Israelites, God's people. Even the plague of darkness, where it was so dark you could feel it. And wherever a person was, they didn't leave that spot for three days. But there was light in all Israel's dwellings.

The people saw these miracles. When they left Egypt, they saw God in a cloud by day and a pillar of fire by night. They had no reason not to believe. They even experienced the miracle at Meribah when God changed the waters from saltwater to freshwater. They even had the manna from heaven. They physically saw God with them. Yet they made this golden calf and went back to their old ways and to what God delivered them from.

The reward or curse of idol-worship can come in many forms. I Samuel 25:3 introduces us to Nabal, a rich man who refused to grant David's request for wages in the form of food. Nabal worshipped the spirit of money. He had no mercy for David or David's men who worked day and night to protect Nabal's servants and his flocks. For this error in judgment, Nabal's reward was a spirit of bitterness and death. If you have had sickness in your body, losses of your finances, or have been brought down to being homeless, think about it. God's laws come with judgments and his love comes with discipline. He loves you, therefore things of judgment and discipline are meant to get you to turn back your heart unto Him.

Let us pray. Lord, I pray for everyone who has been affected by idol worship and has things in their heart that is not pleasing to you. We break every covenant, generational curse, and everything we have spoken to submit ourselves to these gods that are not of you. And we go back to when you rescued us and saved us, and we go back to honoring you. Lord, help us to hear your word. You said that all of your children would hear your voice. Silence every evil voice that is speaking, and let your voice be heard to help us and deliver us. Lord, we repent of our sins and ask for your forgiveness. Show us how to get out of these organizations and break these covenants. Show us how to do good apart from worshipping the devil and calling it you. Help us to truly celebrate your holy days and truly obey your commandments.

Your commandment says to honor the Lord thy God who brought us out of the house of bondage and to have no other gods before you. Lord, if we have broken this commandment, we repent and ask your forgiveness. Thank you, Lord, for sending your mercy. Lord, if you have touched us with sickness, please heal our bodies as we hear you now, Lord, and it won't take much more sickness to get our attention. If you have affected our finances and have allowed the enemy to come and ravish our families, please bless our land. Lord, you said that if my people who are called by my name will repent and submit unto and seek you, then you will heal our land. Lord, we come against every principality and power of the air that is over our houses and our children who are trying to take their lives because of our sin. Lord, we repent in the name of I Am That I Am. If you have allowed thieves to rob us or sent destruction to our home, whatever you have allowed, Lord, you said that you would restore everything that the cankerworm has eaten. Please restore everything that the thief has stolen because of our blindness of not knowing that we were in alignment with them. We command that thief to pay us back double. And Lord, we thank you for your truth.

Chapter 8: Learn From The Holy Days

What's your favorite federal holiday?

_____

I loved Christmas as a child and Valentine's day as a young woman. You may appreciate having Thanksgiving feasts and spending time with family on your paid days off. You may be a person who hates federal holidays altogether.

What's your favorite biblical holiday?

_____

Before I read the bible, I thought that Easter and Christmas were biblical holidays. As a child, each Easter, I received a new Easter basket and new beautiful clothes. I would go to church with my family to hear how Jesus rose on Easter Sunday. The church also preached every December that Christmas was Jesus' birthday. Well, it's nice to celebrate holidays that are also Holy Days, but if only it were Holy Days that honor the Most High God instead of Pagan Gods. Neither Easter bunnies nor Santa Clause is in the bible. Valentine's and Veteran's day aren't there either. The world gives us foolish things to celebrate because our spirit has been made to celebrate and worship God.

For people around the world, the Olympics or the World Cup soccer tournament is a holiday. They are times to have pride land and nation. But God has set up his holydays to not focus on what you are receiving, what nation you should have pride in, nor a day of remembrances of his prophets or the many men and women who fought and died in wars. No, the holy days in the bible are set up with the same mission of why Jesus came. Their purpose is to produce a harvest in you through repentance of sin and turning your heart back to obey the commandments of God so that He might be glorified.

> "...to preach good tiding to the meek, to bind up the brokenhearted, to proclaim liberty to the captives, and the opening of the prison to them that are bound, to proclaim the acceptable year of the Lord, and the day of vengeance of our God, to comfort all who mourn with the garment of praise, that they might be called trees of righteousness, the planting of the Lord that He might be glorified." Isaiah 61:8

If we continue in the mission of Jesus and are managing and charging things to our "Jesus Project," the biblical Holy Days become the weekly, monthly, and quarterly check-ins for how we are progressing in that project. I learned that everyone who believes in Jesus and wants to obey God's commandments is a disciple of Jesus.

The disciples who were with Jesus were not just preaching the gospel. They were making more disciples. John 8:31 "Then said Jesus to those Jews which believed on Him, If ye continue in my word, then are ye my disciples indeed; And ye shall know the truth, and the truth shall make you free." Next,

John 13:34 says, "A new commandment I give unto you, That ye love one another; as I have loved you, that ye also love one another. By this shall all men know that ye are my disciples if ye have love one to another." Finally, John 15:8-10 says, "Herein is my Father glorified, that ye bear much fruit; so shall ye be my disciples. As the Father hath loved me, so have I loved you: continue ye in my love; If ye keep my commandments, ye shall abide in my love; even as I have kept my Fathers' commandments, and abide in his love."

Jesus said that He came to do the will of his father. Furthermore, in St. John 20:21, Jesus said, "...Peace be unto you: as my Father hath sent me, even so, send I you." If you want to be saved, you should continue in Jesus' mission. He says that whatever His father sent Him to do, He's sending you to do. This mission can also be found in Luke 4:18. It reads, "The Spirit of the Lord is upon me because He hath anointed me to preach the gospel to the poor; He hath sent me to heal the brokenhearted, to preach deliverance to the captives, and to recover sight to the blind, to set at liberty them that are bruised, and to preach the acceptable year of the Lord. And He closed the book, and He gave it again to the minister and sat down. And the eyes of all them that were in the synagogue were fastened on him. And He began to say unto them; This day is this scripture fulfilled in your ears."

Jesus stated his mission for us to follow in Luke 4:18. What was He reading from? Jesus was reading scripture from the book of Isaiah 61:1. If our mission is to do what Jesus did, we need to understand each part of the mission. Let's break down what each line of the mission means.

I The Spirit of the Lord is upon me – Who was the spirit of Lord upon? We need to prove that Jesus is the Messiah.

A: Genesis 3:15, And I will put enmity because thee and the woman. Her seed shall bruise thy head, and thou shall bruise his heel. The men of Israel will somehow be empowered to rule over Satan's seed through the deliverance of one of their brethren, the Messiah.

B: Deuteronomy 18:18, I will raise them a prophet from among their brethren like unto thee and put my words in His mouth. And He shall speak unto them all that I command Him. And it shall come to past that whosoever shall not hearken to my words He shall speak in my name I will require it of him. Who is this profit? **The Messiah**.

C: Psalms 91:1, Sing unto the Lord a new song for He has done marvelously. His right hand and His holy arm has gotten Him the victory. **The Messiah is also described as the Holy Arm of the Lord.**

D: Psalms 77:15, Thou hath with thine Arm redeemed thy people the sons of Jacob and Joseph. **Some redeemer is coming called the arm of the Lord; he is the messiah.**

E: Jeremiah 30:9, But they shall serve the Lord their God and David their king who I will raise unto them.

F: Ezekiel 34:29, And will raise for them a Plant of renowned and they shall no longer be consumed with hunger in the land and bear the shame of the heathen any more. **A savior is coming.**

G: Isaiah 51:3, Who has believed our report and to whom is the Arm of the Lord revealed? For He shall grow up before Him as a tender plant and as a root out of the dry ground. He has no form or comeliness, and when we see Him, there is no beauty that we should desire. He is despised and rejected by men. A man of sorrows and acquainted with grief, and we hide as it were our faces from Him. He was despised, and we esteemed Him not. **Who are all these prophets talking about? They are speaking about the Messiah to come.**

H: Isaiah 53:12, He was numbered with the transgressors and bear the sin of many.

I: Matthew 1:16, And Jacob begot Joseph the husband of Mary of whom was born Jesus who is called Christ. **Finally, this Christ or this Messiah has come.**

He is the one whom all these prophets from Genesis to Matthew have prophesized about. It's Him who the Spirit of the Lord is upon. It's upon the Messiah, Jesus, so that He can do all these things to free His people, the children of Israel, to defeat the children of Satan.

Now, if the spirit of the Lord is upon Jesus, is the spirit of the Lord also upon his disciples? How do we get the Holy Spirit? Luke 11:13 If ye being evil to know how to give good gifts to your children, how much more shall your heavenly Father give the Holy Spirit to them that ask Him. Acts 2:1, "When the day of Pentecost was fully come, they were all with one accord and in one place. And they were all filled with the Holy Ghost." Acts 8:14, "Now, when the apostles who were at Jerusalem heard that Samaria received the word of God, they sent unto them Peter and John, who when they were come down, prayed for them that they might receive the Holy Ghost. For as yet, He was fallen upon none of them. Only they were baptized in the name of the Lord Jesus. Then they laid their hands on them, and they received the Holy Ghost." The laying on the hands is one way to receive the Holy Ghost. Then we learned in Acts 10:44 that While Peter yet spake these words, the Holy Ghost fell on all them who heard the word. Peter was speaking to a group of Gentiles, and as he was preaching to them, the gospel message The Holy Ghost came upon and fell on the people who heard the words. As a disciple, you can receive the Holy Ghost. And you can pray for others to receive the Holy Ghost or lay hands on them.

II Preach the gospel or good tidings to the meek – Sin and death were our rewards because the wages of sin is death. When Adam sinned, every seed inside him was subject to death, and our land was defiled. But because of the Messiah's birth and sacrifice, we can have everlasting life, power over our enemies, and rest from fear, sorrow, and hard bondage. It takes repentance, baptism, and obeying the commandments of God.

The gospel message also says that there will be a huge earthquake to shake the heavens and earth. This earth will be destroyed by fire. Isaiah 24:1-26. There will be a day of darkness when our savior returns to root out his enemies, including Satan, death, and every nation which opposed Israel. Then the light will arise on God's people, and they will be gathered from everywhere on Earth that they are scattered and brought to our new and glorious home Zion. We will be married to the Lord, and our land will be married to us. All other nations will bless us and serve us in righteousness. This information and more concerning the gospel message can be found in the book of Isaiah, chapters 13-61

John 3:3 Except a man be born again, he cannot see the kingdom of God. Verily, verily I say unto thee except a man be born of water, and of the spirit, he cannot enter into the kingdom of God. John 3:14 says and as Moses lifted the serpent in the wilderness, even so, must the Son of man be lifted that whosoever believeth in Him shall not perish but have eternal life.

John the Baptist also spoke in Matthew 3:8 Bring therefore fruits meet for repentance, and now also the ax is laid at the root of the trees. Therefore, every tree which bringeth forth not good fruit is hewn down and cast into the fire. I indeed baptize you with water unto repentance, but He that cometh after me is mightier than I, He shall baptize you with the Holy Ghost and with fire. Whose fan is in His hand, and He will thoroughly purge his floor and garner His wheat into the garner, but He will burn up the chaff with unquenchable fire.

How do we become wheat and not chaff? We must repent of our sins, then give to those in need and minister to others with our gifts and talents. This is how we produce fruit.

The proof of this can be found in Matthew 25:32. Jesus tells the story of what He will do when He returns. He says He will gather all nations and divide His sheep from the goats. The sheep are called blessed by His Father and are invited to inherit the kingdom prepared for them. For he says that when He was hungry, they gave Him meat. When He was thirsty, they gave Him a drink, and when He was a stranger, they took Him in. When He was naked, they clothed Him. When He was sick, they visited Him. And when He was in prison, they came to see Him. Jesus explains that when the righteous did these things to the least of people, they were doing it unto Him. To the goats, He commanded them to depart from Him into everlasting fire which confirms what John the Baptist preached. The goats did not help the poor or minister to others with their gifts and talents.

The sheep of the Lord are blessed with eternal life, and not just after death; they are rich on earth because of their commitment to doing. Revelation 2:9 I know thy tribulation and thy poverty, but thou are rich. God's people appear to be poor, but they are rich. And not just rich in heaven, rich on Earth. I have another teaching on how to stop the enemy from stealing your blessings so that they physically manifest for you.

Furthermore, Matthew 5 says blessed are the poor in spirit, for theirs is the kingdom of heaven. Blessed are they that mourn, for they shall be comforted. Blessed are the meek, for they shall inherit the earth. Blessed are they which do hunger and thirst after righteousness, for they shall be filled. Blessed are ye when men shall revile you and persecute you and say all manner of evil against you for my sake. Rejoice and be exceeding glad for great is your reward in heaven. For so persecuted the profits which were before ye.

How else do we preach the gospel to the poor? Isaiah 53:4 says, surely He has born our grief and carried our sorrows thou He was wounded for our transgressions, and He was bruised for our iniquities, and with His stripes, we are healed. We let them know that they are healed in the Lord.

III Heal the brokenhearted – In order to accomplish this task, we tell people the truth. That God especially cares about people who are hurting. Psalms 102:17 says, "He will regard the prayer of the destitute, and not despise their prayer." Psalms 34:17 The righteous cry and the Lord heareth and delivereth them out of all their troubles. The Lord is nigh unto them that are of a broken heart and saveth such as be of a contrite spirit. Psalms 37:25, I have been young and now am old. I have not seen the righteous forsaken nor his seed begging bread. Luke 6:22, Blessed are ye when men shall hate you and when they shall separate you from their company and shall reproach you and cast out your name as evil for the son of man's sake. Shall I go on? We have a series of scriptures to give people hope when they are brokenhearted. Let them know that they are not alone and that God hears them and will comfort them.

IV Proclaim liberty to the captives – First, we need to understand who is a captive and what they are bound with. Isaiah 42:7, "To bring out the prisoners from the prison and them that sit in darkness out of the prison houses." Let's hear what Jesus said about being captive. In John 8:33, Jesus was speaking with the Pharisees, and they answered Him, "We be Abraham's seed, and we were never in bondage to any man. How sayeth thou ye shall be made free?" Jesus answered them, "Verily, verily I say unto you whosoever committeth sin is the servant of sin and a servant abideth not in the house forever but the son abideth forever." Anyone who is serving sin by committing sins is in bondage to sin. You are a servant of sin, and a servant does not abide in the house forever.

You have to free yourself from the servitude of sin. Ecclesiastes 4:13 says, "Better is a poor and a wise child than an old and foolish king who will no more be admonished for out of prison he cometh to reign whereas also he that is born in his kingdom becometh poor." Even if you are a very powerful person on this Earth, you can still be in bondage if you refuse to be corrected.

The bible also teaches that the poor also refuse to be corrected. Anyone in the kingdom of this foolish king shall come to poverty. Psalms 16:10 For thou will not leave my soul in hell. Psalms 49:15 But God will redeem my soul from the power of the grave. We shall have everlasting life and not in bondage to sin. Job 19:25 says, "For I know that my redeemer liveth."

Who is the redeemer? The Messiah was anointed to come and preach to the captives. Isaiah 44:6 "Thus saith the Lord the king of Israel and his redeemer the Lord of hosts, I am the first, and I am the last, and besides me, there is no God." Psalms 130:8 says, "And He shall redeem Israel from all of his Inequities."

Hebrews 2:14 "For as much then as the children are partakers of flesh and blood, He also Himself took part of the same that through death He might destroy him that had the power of death that is the devil and deliver them who through fear of death were all their lifetime subject to bondage."

We were subject to bondage because of sin from the very first sin, but now we have a redeemer who will not leave our souls in hell. Leviticus 16:34, "And this shall be an everlasting statute unto you to make an atonement for the children of Israel for all their sins once a year." There has always been a law to make sure that Israel is redeemed for their sins.

Now we have a redeemer in our Lord Jesus, who is now our High Priest in heaven. To make atonement for us. He sacrificed his body as a sin offering for us to be free. We give all the curses meant for our lives to Him because He became a curse for us. And we put on His righteousness and take on His yoke, which is light and easy. I John 3:4 Whosoever committeth sin transgresseth also the law for sin is the transgression of the law.

As we said in the beginning, whoever commits sin is the servant of sin. You are in bondage and need to be set free by being redeemed through repentance and transferring that sin to the blood our Lord shed for us. In Luke 13:16, Jesus is talking, and there is a bunch of people around Him, and He says, "And ought not this woman, being a daughter of Abraham, whom Satan hath bound, lo, these eighteen years, be loose from this bond on the Sabbath Day." This woman was bound and couldn't sit up straight. Her back was arched over.

Many people of God are bound with sickness, disease, curses, etc., many from sins, generational curses, demonic attacks, idol worship, etc. But we can break these curses off our lives and break them by preaching deliverance to the captives. We have a right to health on Earth with the power Jesus gives us to rule over evil spirits.

I have been healed of depression, anxiety, and chronic back pain. I have prayed for people to be healed of pains and many ailments in their bodies, and they were too healed. Evil spirits work to bind believers, especially with sickness and disease, delay, anger, confusion, etc. But by the power of the Most High God and by obeying his commandments, we can be delivered.

V Preach the acceptable year of the Lord – We are commanded as Disciples to tell both the good and the bad. The blessings and the curses. Some ministers get a lot of criticism because they mostly talk about all the good blessings that are coming your way. But Jesus said that we must speak about the Day of the Lord, his coming back, the days of darkness when the sun won't shine, and the darkness can be felt, the earthquake that will occur when He shakes the heavens, and the killings that He will make on that day.

Many profits in the Old Testament spoke about this Day of the Lord. The book of Isaiah says, "For the day of the Lord of

Hosts shall be upon every one that is proud and lofty and upon every one that is lifted up and he shall be brought low." This day of the Lord is not going to be a good thing for people with pride in their hearts or those who feel superior to others.

Isaiah 13:6 says, "Howl ye for the day of the Lord is at hand. It shall come as destruction from the almighty therefore shall all hands be faint and every man's heart shall melt and they shall be afraid. Pains and sorrows shall take hold of them. They shall be in pain as a woman that travelleth. They shall be amazed one at another. Their faces shall be flames.

Isaiah 13:9 goes on to say, "Behold, the day of the Lord cometh cruel, both with wrath and fierce anger to lay the land desolate, and He shall destroy the sinner thereof out of it. For the stars of heaven and the constellations thereof shall not give their light. The sun shall be darkened in his going forth, and the moon shall not cause her light to shine. And I will punish the world for their evil and the wicked for their iniquity, and I will cause the arrogancy of the proud to cease and will lay low the haughtiness of the terrible. I will shake the heavens and the earth and remove them out of her place. Their children also shall be dashed into pieces before their eyes." Acts 2:20, "The sun shall be turned into darkness and the moon into blood before that great and notable day of the Lord came.

Here are more reference scriptures for you to learn about this day of the Lord to preach the acceptable year of the Lord. Be a good disciple and look them up to teach this message to those that the Lord leads you to. Jeremiah 46:10; Ezekiel 13:5, 30:3; Joel 1:15, 2:1-31; Amos 5:18-20; Obadiah 1:15; Zephaniah 1-14; Zechariah 14:1; Malachi 4:5

♦♦♦

Communing with God can also be done by keeping God's Feasts throughout the year. These Holy days and Feast days are different from holidays in the world because like His commandments, Feast days have a deeper and secret meaning. Each Holy day reveals something about how to have a stronger relationship with Him, the end times, salvation, or redemption. We grow closer to reproducing after his image by practicing on Earth the Holy Days that he has ordained in heaven.

When I read about the Sabbath Day and the Feast of the Passover, I immediately started trying to figure out which calendar day they should be celebrated. Later I learned about the Feast of First Fruits & Tabernacles and all the rest of the holy days. After almost eight months of confusion, listening to this blog or that one, looking at what Jewish people are doing, watching this video, or reading that book in order to figure it out, I still wasn't sure. All I knew for certain was that a day ends when the sun goes down, and the beginning of the year was in the Spring and not the New Year's Day that we typically celebrated by watching the ball drop in New York City. It took an intervention of the Holy Spirit to help me.

The Holy Spirit spoke in my ear and revealed to me to simply take the day of the year when the sunlight was the same length as the darkness. Twelve hours of light and 12 hours of darkness. The Book of Enoch says that on that day of equal light and darkness, in the Springtime, is the last day of the year. The New Year starts on the following day. That was the clue that I needed. Everything else, or almost everything else, made sense after that. God's calendar was revealed to me. 13 weeks Spring, 13 weeks Summer, 13 weeks Fall, and 13 weeks Winter. The sun either gives light or decreases light following a pattern of:

Spring: 30 days, 30 days, 31 days;

Summer: 30 days, 30 days, 31 days;

Fall: 30 days, 30 days, 31 days;

Winter: 30 days, 30 days, 31 days;

This is why we are told in Genesis 1:14, "And God said, Let there be lights in the firmament of the heaven to divide the day from the night, and let them be for signs, and seasons, and days, and years." Now don't go trying to look up the date that the Equinox falls on because it is not a date of equal light or darkness. I went to a website called timeanddate.com to research the days of the year where there are 12 hours of sunlight. March 17th, or what the world celebrates as St. Patrick's Day, is usually the true New Year's date. Therefore, March 16th is the day of 12 hours of light and 12 hours of darkness.

I have been very blessed with emotional experiences with keeping these Holy Days. In keeping the Passover and Feast of Unleavened Bread, I have learned just how the smallest amount of sin in my life could defile me, put me in the camp of Satan, and block my blessings. In keeping the Feast of Tabernacles, where you sleep in a tent for a week, I learned to let go of fear, not complain about my situation, and have more faith in God. In keeping the Feast of the First Fruits, I learned about the servants of God and to honor Him with my first so that He will bless the rest. In keeping the weekly Sabbath days, I've learned to trust Him as my provider and that one day, I will have a long rest to enjoy.

Let's review where to find the Holy Day Laws & summarize their calendar schedule for your understanding. The laws can be found in: Leviticus 23; Exodus 13; Numbers 28

- All the feasts are holy convocations
- The 7th day each week is the Sabbath day, and no work can be done
- Proclaim the Feasts in their season
- The 14th day of the 1st month at even is the Lord's Passover
- The 15th day of the same month is the Feast of Unleavened Bread for seven days, where you eat unleavened bread each day.

- The Feast of the First Fruits is on the 1st day of each season, 1st day of 1st month, 4th month, 7th month, 10th month, and on the day of Pentecost.
- Keep the day of Pentecost. It is one plus seven sabbaths after the initial first fruits offering or 50 days. Do no servile work and have a holy convocation on each of these days.
- The 1st day of the 7th month is the Feast of Trumpets, where you blow trumpets
- The Day of Atonement is the 9th day of the 7th month from even to even, and there is a fast of no food or drink.
- The 15th day of the 7th month is the Feast of Tabernacles for seven days where ye dwell in booths

The book of Esther adds another couple of feasts day entitled Purim. And the Apocrypha book of 2 Maccabees adds another week of Feast days in the winter called the Feast of Dedication of the altar, which Jesus also kept, as evident in John 10:22.

I'm going to reveal to you what God has revealed to me about each holy day.

A. Sabbath Day – This time is a weekly reminder that God has promised to give us rest. Think about what is rest? Is there anything we can do forever? We can't sleep forever because that causes bed sores. We can't stay woke forever because that causes exhaustion, and we'll fall out. We can't stand forever or lie down forever. We are in a state of constant motion, a little here and a little there. Where is the rest or final peace?

I read in other historical books that the Sabbath represents the day that God rested in the book of Genesis. All the time that He created has been divided up according to the seven days mentioned in Genesis. Each day is 1000 years of the total time that will exist. Adam was told that if He ate from the tree of Good and Evil, he would die that day. Genesis 5:5 says that "And all the days that Adam lived were nine hundred and thirty years: and he died." Adam died on the day he was created because he did not live forever in his flesh or past the first 1000 years. God did not personally reveal this day theory to me, but I have no reason to refute it.

For your "Jesus project," check in each week to reflect on your sins, personal goals, and progress on becoming the best version of yourself. Check in to reflect on how many souls you have let your light shine on. Think about the people who asked you for help. Think about your progress in discerning good from evil. Count the number of your prayers that have been answered this week and give God praise. Use this time to check in with God's servants and the poor of his kingdom.

B. Feast of the 1st Fruits – This holy day represents a reminder to give to the poor, widows, strangers, the fatherless, and God's servants. For your "Jesus project," pray and write down the names of God's servants, people in your life who you can personally bless with something. Since I like to bake, I made cakes and gave them to people the Holy Spirit revealed to me as his servants. Also, give to God's people on this day: strangers, the poor in your land, widows, and the fatherless children. Remember to check in with these people throughout the year.

C. Passover – On this holy day, God told the Children of Israel to take the blood of a lamb and smear it on their doorposts, so when the death angel came, He would see the blood on the door and Passover the house. Our faith in Jesus allows us to be covered by his blood and righteousness. When the death angel sees us, he'll see the righteousness of Jesus covering us and "pass over" us. For your "Jesus Project," put away fear and know that you are covered with his righteous blood. Boldly ask for everything you need to be who you were meant to be without condemnation or hesitation. Remember to focus on your "what" and "why" versus how it will get done. Remember not to focus on your past sins, your background, or your mistakes because all is forgiven, and you now have a project to help others in the name of Jesus.

D. Feast of Unleavened Bread – This holy day shows us how we need not eat from the tree of Good and Evil. We have to focus on the truth of God and continuously cast down the smallest untruthful thought, condemning thought, or judgmental thought that enters our minds. Our thoughts are what defiles us. Jesus says in Mark 7:20-23, "That which cometh out of the man, that defileth the man. For from within, out of the heart of man, proceed evil thoughts, adulteries, fornications, murders, thefts, covetousness, wickedness, deceit, lasciviousness, an evil eye, blasphemy, pride, foolishness: All these evil things come from within, and defile the man." For your "Jesus Project," think about all the negative thoughts that have come into your mind and cast them down. Dissociate yourself from the spiritual enemies who want you to agree with them. Check your heart for any grudges or judgments you are holding against anyone. Repent for anything that comes to your heart.

E: The day of Pentecost – The Lord can reverse the curse He set at the tower of Babel and give you supernatural powers to speak a different language in order to spread the truth of the gospel message to his children. For your "Jesus Project," consider the people you have been able to minister to. Consider how God was able to use you to spread the truth of his kingdom. Be joyful for others being able to improve their lives or gain hope because of you. Put away fear and look at the people you work with or encounter and identify if you are the blessing sent to sustain and encourage them.

F: The Feast of Trumpets – When the Lord returns after the days of darkness, where just like in Egypt, He will send thick darkness to cover the Earth, a darkness that will be felt, He is going to blow a loud trumpet in the Earth and gather his children together. For your "Jesus Project," purchase a trumpet and blow it every Sabbath day and Holy Day. Remember that the Lord is coming back to take vengeance on his enemies and restore everything for our good. Be joyous and enjoy your Holy Days.

G: Day of Atonement – Jesus is now our high priest. Any activities that were performed by a Levite or High Priest have been transferred to Jesus in Heaven. For your "Jesus Project," understand that there are consequences for sin and consequences for repentance. Yes, we should mourn and feel bad when we repent. We don't want to play with God making the same mistakes over and over again. Being lukewarm will not do. God allows us to lose things that are valuable to us to teach us to be sorry about how we treat people. Sometimes, we have to feel the loss of the things that we care about. Have mercy on those who can't pay you back. Don't participate in the slander news culture that we live in. Let go of the fear of others trying to attack you. Remove all leaven from your heart. Our sins can be atoned for if we acknowledge them, feel bad about them and turn our hearts away from them forever.

H: Feast of Tabernacles – Hard times are coming, just like when the children of Israel lived in tents. But we are not meant to complain or be in fear, but to trust God as our loving father who will feed us, give us drink, and deliver us to his promised place of Zion. For your "Jesus Project" in a troubled time, request the supplies you need. Request wisdom and resources for how to navigate the storm. Have faith that you shall receive everything you need. Remember that when there was no food in the wilderness, God rained bread from heaven and gave water from the rock.

You will discover your lessons by following these holy days. You will see your life and understanding of life shift from how the world celebrates holidays. My prayer is that you are blessed in your new experiences.

Chapter 9: Conclusion

Being a Christian and believing in Jesus does not mean that you are no longer cursed. It means that you now have a pathway to Salvation. But that road could be filled with misery or blessings depending on if you choose to obey the commandments of God or ignore them.

I was a Christian who believed in the son of God for my salvation, yet because of my actions and my ignorance, I was not participating in the slew of blessings that God has promised to those who love and obey Him. Understand that the word of God is alive, and He was made flesh. His name in the bible is Jesus. Just like He is alive, so are your words that go out of your mouth. Your words will bring you back whatever you send them to do, just like Jesus will bring his father back the things that He is sent to do.

Position yourself to receive your blessing by not putting your trust in a man or a government program. Trust that when you speak your "what" and your "why" in the name of Jesus, you will have whatever you spoke. Be who you were meant to be and bless God by blessing his servants, his poor, his widows, his fatherless children, and strangers.

Your body is the temple of the Holy Spirit. Our hearts and our minds are the altars of sacrifice to the Lord. Will you bless unclean food in the name of the Lord and eat it with your mouth? Or will you speak words that curse your own life (I'm broke, I don't have a job, I'm poor) and accept these thoughts in your mind? As I learned the deeper meaning of the commandments and as I broke away from our traditions of eating unclean things and thinking unclean thoughts, I began to hear from God clearer, and my life improved.

About the Author

Tamara Keeler is a walking inspiration. She has helped non-profits, for-profits, and individuals to achieve their goals using a lean steward mindset. She believes that every person has a God given business inside of them waiting to be produced. Her business, I Am Lean LLC was set up to fulfill that long term vision.

Tamara makes biblical concepts easy to understand. People often tell her that they avoided lean and using the King James Bible before hearing her teach them. Tamara does not believe that business should be separate from religion. She teaches how to use biblical principles and lean concepts to grow your business.

Tamara is from the west side of Chicago and was a teen mom. She had more opposition than support while working, trying to graduate high school, then attend college. She often felt discouraged as a mom going to class after class and working until close at Home Depot. But she never stopped. She set a standard when there was no one in her family that could even relate to what she was going through or where she was headed. She inspired her daughters to be great. The sacrifices she made for her Black daughters for the past 20 years have allowed them to have the same opportunities as their White peers who had parents with 10x the resources and time and support systems. Tamara's youngest daughter, 22, just secured a top paying job with Google. Through stints of homelessness, food scarcity, mental ailments, and racism, Tamara has learned why she has experienced the various levels of pain and prosperity. Tamara's story is truly one of going from living cursed to blessed.